Table of Contents

I0026704

THE MYSTERY OF CHOCTAW RIDGE

A COLLECTION OF SHORT STORIES

by
Janson Mancheski

Copyright © 2023 by Janson Mancheski
All Rights Reserved. No part of this publication may be reproduced, distributed, or transmitted in any form or by any means, including photocopying, recording, or other electronic or mechanical methods, without the author or publisher's prior written permission.

Author's Opening Note:

The stories here are all works of fiction. Most originated as stand-alone short stories and were later absorbed as scenes or episodes in my "The Chemist Series" novels. It often amuses me how a simple idea can manifest into a few storylines, which transform into a poem; the poem provides the theme for a short fiction story. This story often expands into a premise for a novel or movie script. A string of books containing similar surroundings and characters can evolve into an adventure series. This concept is a well-known trope. It's been around since Aesop composed his first fable. It also conveys how tiny acorns may someday transform into giant oak trees or how little train locomotives become mighty engines by convincing themselves: "I think I can; I think I can."

INTRODUCTION

A friend one day asked why I was composing a book of short stories. My answer was simple. As an early reader of Ernest Hemingway, I recalled being drawn toward his short stories more than his novels. As a novice composer of poems and naughty limericks to amuse my friends, I imagined short fiction could be composed in a single day. Often, this assumption proved correct in my tall-tale attempts. Of course, the initial draft never consumes the most time—it's the rereads, polishing, tweaking, and rewrites. All are essentials before the piece is complete. First then can it be shipped off for third-party assessment.

Nevertheless, authoring condensed stories is far less tedious than composing novels—especially series novels. With this in mind, I accepted that I had a short fiction tome inside me aching for release. I never imagined a half-baked memoir might emerge from the project.

Everyone has their personal writing methods and ambitions. After penning stories for years, one's strengths and weaknesses become evident. In my case, I've always defined myself as an "ideas writer." I have a continuous flow of thoughts regarding characters, plots, movie visions, methods of deviance, ideas for plot lines, et cetera. While working on a story, my brain often volunteers many What Ifs. More often than not, these ideas aren't relevant to the story I'm composing but are out-of-the-blue flashes about other plots—ones I've promised myself I'll someday write.

Consequently, I jot these ideas down on little random slips of paper. They are stuffed inside folders and envelopes, paperclipped together—character names, concepts, overviews, and other whatnot—that I've decided might someday evolve into a story, much like the little engine that could.

Point Two: Secondarily, one of my other fascinations centers around the inevitability of death.

I imagined this was due to my early love of science fiction and murder mysteries. I felt curiously drawn to the works of E.A. Poe and H.P. Lovecraft. Reading their works forces one to ponder one's final demise. Yet, this wasn't the primary driver. Another reason for composing this book of short tales is due to actual incidents that have happened during my life. I've become fascinated—perhaps even morbidly—by how many times I've survived within

5

inches of dying. And why these had occurred. I recall in minutia how each one happened.

Consequently, I can list over a dozen times when I might have perished, but for the grace of God. As time passed, I compiled the what, when, where, and even why these events had happened. Like the detectives who color my crime thriller stories, the puzzle intrigued me.

So, what does all this have to do with short stories? While deciding which tales to include in this book, it struck me that these near-death episodes might be exciting additions. They'd engage the readers and reveal what I meant by their occurrences. Thus, another dilemma arose: What should I call these episodes? How best to refer to them? I couldn't describe them as Near-Death Experiences (NDEs). I hadn't died or experienced any out-of-body travel. My soul hadn't fled my flesh and followed a light tunnel into the spiritual realm. No, I had merely survived numerous life-or-death incidents.

Of course, many of us have survived similar situations—where the result may have ended our lives within inches or seconds. Every fall, car accident, choking, deep cut, burn, animal attack, medical error. . . or other potentially life-threatening events have happened to many of us. Yet, in my case—having documented close to twenty of these episodes—they seemed to defy probability unless you're Evil Kinevil, a NASCAR racer, snake handler, or mercenary soldier.

I've wrestled with assigning these incidents a proper euphemism or acronym. "Nearly died," "Close call," "Saved by an angel," "Narrow escape," et cetera. And dozens of other similar combinations to see if any stuck. As a result, I've decided to refer to these occurrences as "Almost Died Events." (ADEs) The medical profession uses "Close calls." My episodes remain different from Near-Death Experiences (NDEs). My ADEs never caused temporary dying, no drifting toward a light tunnel or experiencing an OBE. I vividly recall occasions when time slowed during the event, and my thoughts became laser-focused. And yet, for reasons unknown, some miracle tipped the odds in my favor, and I survived. If my episodes land inside the present NDE parameters, so be it. It makes no difference one way or the other.

As a result, I've compiled these episodes within this text chronologically, writing them as vignettes among my other short stories. They may not be interesting to everyone (other than as short stories). Still, I also imagine that a certain percentage of readers here might have also experienced times when they came within inches of biting the bullet.

In conclusion, I hope you'll find these real-life tales somewhat amusing or intriguing—hopefully, both. I'd also enjoy hearing about your personal ADE incidents—either lighthearted or deadly serious.

Sincerely,

JM

PS: Who, while penning this, remains actively in the present. At least for the time being, anyway.

This book is dedicated to my guardian angel, Toni, whom I recently assigned as a *female* guardian angel. I named her Toni, as a proper name, because I've had to thank her many times over the years for saving my bacon. When voicing my thanks aloud—mostly at home alone or sometimes while driving—I've often felt awkward when addressing her as "Guardian angel." It's how thanking the "Holy Ghost" sometimes feels distant. As a result, she's now "Toni" (though I assume angels are genderless). Nevertheless, I trust that Toni isn't offended by my bestowing her a human name—thus personalizing our relationship. The point is, I want to thank you, Toni, from my heart's bottom, for all the times you've saved me from several what could have been gruesome deaths.

MY CHRONOLOGICAL LIST OF ALMOST DIED EVENTS

Almost Died Event # 1 – CLOTHESLINE CHOKE – age 8

Almost Died Event # 2 – BURN OR DROWN – age 12

Almost Died Event # 3 – SWING BLADE – age 13

Almost Died Event # 4 – LOCKER DEATH TRAP – age 14

Almost Died Event # 5 – BRAIN BLEED – age 18

Almost Died Event # 6 – FATAL BOTTLE ROCKET – age 18

Almost Died Event # 7 – DOOR COUNTY WHIZZERS – age 18

Almost Died Event # 8 – ROTC STRAY BULLET – age 19

Almost Died Event # 9 – FEDERAL OFFENSE. – age 20

Almost Died Event # 10 – SHOOTING BLANKS – age 20

(Likely not a true ADE, but in this day and age, a SWAT team would have surrounded the dormitory in minutes.)

Almost Died Event # 11 – DORM WINDOW DROP – age 20

Almost Died Event # 12 – BLIND STAIRWELL – age 20

Almost Died Event # 13 –SHOOTING WYATT EARP – age 20

(If authorities had been summoned to calls of "Shots fired," things would have ended badly for the pranksters.)

Almost Died Event # 14 – HEAD-ON COLLISION – age 40

Almost Died Event # 15 – SPEEDING DRUNK– Age 45

Almost Died Event # 16 – DARK NIGHT TURNOFF – Age 46

Almost Died Event # 17 – JOY OF HYDROPLANING – age 48.

The above ADEs are all true. I've listed them chronologically for conciseness. While a few can be considered as close calls (the medical term for almost perishing), which many of us may have experienced during our lifetimes, what stands out to me are the narrow escapes I've survived. Thus, I've defined them as Almost Died Events. (ADEs). When you've narrowly escaped death nearly twenty times, you begin paying attention to how fortunate you are to be upright and breathing.

So there we have it. And once again, my utmost and heartfelt thank you to my fantastic Guardian Angel, Toni. May God bless.

Author's Note: Please email me your personal "Almost Died Events" if you choose. The e-mail address is also listed on this book's final page. Peace, love, prosperity.

— JM (drjjjjdr@yahoo.com)

Almost Died Event # 1 – CLOTHESLINE CHOKE – age 8

I was eight years old and lived in Sturgeon Bay, Wisconsin. My neighbor Bobby lived down the hill on the other side of a mid-block alley. We were goofing around that sunny afternoon. I ignored my regular bike and scooter'd an old tricycle beneath my mom's four hanging clotheslines. Standing atop the seat, I grabbed the two inside lines, one in each hand. I crossed them and slipped my head between them to make Bobby laugh. The tricycle began rolling down the hill. Trapped, holding on by the toe of my Keds, I shouted, "Bobby! Go get my mom!" He stiffly replied, "I'm not going inside your house by myself." Hearing my shouts, my mom emerged from the garage to see what we were up to this time.

THE MYSTERY
OF CHOCTAW RIDGE

Logline: When a teenage girl becomes pregnant by an older boy, her family unites to help solve the problem and escape judgment by a close-minded Sothern community in the 1960s.

Themes: young love, community judgment, Southern Baptists, frontier justice, buried secrets.

Plot summary: 1965. A rural Mississippi community is shocked to learn that a young man leaped off a local bridge in an apparent suicide attempt. Though some residents raised their eyebrows, Choctaw County officials recorded the death as a self-inflicted drowning.

1965, Central Mississippi – Choctaw Ridge
May 28, Friday

Lara peeked from beneath her straw hat at the scorching sun, which blazed with the brassy shimmer of a high-hat cymbal. The heat seared the rolling hills and thousands of acres of cotton, hay, and soybean fields. Lara held a half-filled burlap sack of plucked cotton, wearing bleached bib overalls and high-top tennis shoes. Thirty yards away, her father and brother Ray tightened hay bales before hoisting them into the wooden back of the flatbed truck.

Papa wore his dark, weather-beaten hat. Ray wore cotton suspender pants and a beige work shirt—his usual attire. The sun's heat was getting to Lara. Her skin felt pale, forehead flushed. Unable to stand the heat anymore, she dropped her sack and ran twenty yards into the trees at the edge of the field, disappearing.

Sensing the commotion behind them, the men turned and watched her flee from view.

Papa asked, "What the devil?"

"Could be a rattler, Papa. Copperheads mostly run from our noise."

"She'd scream if she got bit."

They stared at the forest where Lara had disappeared, waiting for her to emerge. After two minutes, Papa said, "Better go see what's wrong, boy."

Ray tossed his gloves aside. He strode briskly across the hayfield's edge and crossed the strip of cotton field, disappearing into the trees where his younger

12

sister had vanished. He located Lara in a clearing fifteen feet in. She knelt on the ground between two box elders and a birch stand. The birds had gone silent with the intruder's presence, and the sudden shade felt soothing to the boy.

He approached Lara quietly, though she recognized his footsteps. The girl knelt with hands upon knees, her face sweaty and flushed. Her hat was tossed aside. There was clumpy, beige-colored moisture on the weedy ground in front of her, and Ray recognized the detritus of her expelled breakfast. He slipped alongside and massaged her narrow shoulder. Lara flinched but didn't look up.

"Flu bug, maybe? Or the heat get to ya?"

"Something I ate. The heat sure ain't helping none."

Ray stooped down to her level. He peeled a strand of cattail weed and slid it between his teeth. "I know a BS line when I hear it. You've gained ten pounds in the last two months, Lara." He added, "Working in this heat, you shoulda lost near as much."

Lara shook her head, disappointed. Her voice was a husky whisper. "Something I ate is all." A hiccup escaped her puffy lips. She glanced at her brother. "Tell Papa I'll be out in a minute."

Ray chewed on the weed. "I hate it, but got to ask—how far along are you?" He watched her cringe. "You know they'll suspect baby sickness. So you got to fess up about matters."

Lara kept her head lowered. "Three months now." Glancing his way, her eyes pleaded: "Please don't say nothing, Ray. I can work just fine. I can't let on—"

"They're not stupid."

Lara sobbed and buried her face in her hands, ashamed her secret was now out.

Ray tossed his weed aside and touched her shoulder gently. "Come on. Get back to work, or Papa will throw a fit. He reached beneath her arm and assisted her to her feet. As they neared the forest edge, Lara said, "This blasted heat sets my insides to wrestling."

"I'll tell him it's the heat. Long as you can pull your weight, he won't get too riled."

They emerged from the woods and strode together across the field. Papa eyed them suspiciously and said, "It's about time. I thought of calling the County Sheriff for a search party."

Ray said, "Female problems, I guess."

Papa frowned, the deep creases narrowing his eyes. "Hoist that bale up, boy. We still got this section to finish. Then, days from now, we'll get to those last five acres on the lower forty." He stared across at Lara as she resumed picking cotton. He called out: "And you, young lady. We're gonna have us a chat this evening after dinner.

"Yes, Papa."

Nightfall arrived soon after supper. Momma sent Lara outside to gather kindling, and Ray accompanied her. There had been recent reports of wolves in the area attacking a nearby farmer's chicken coop, and being six years older, Ray was handier with Papa's .45 pistol.

They walked silently to the edge of the yard. Light exuded from the farmhouse behind them. Lara carried a canvas satchel and a flashlight. She flicked it on as she stepped inside the woods at the west edge of their yard. They heard an animal skidder and run for cover.

Ray asked, "Are you feeling better?"

Lara nodded. "I thought about what you said earlier, Ray. You're right. It'll all come out sooner or later."

"Billy Joe McCallister, isn't it?" She didn't look his way and walked ahead. Ray added, "He'll pay the medical bills, won't he? If you get it quick-fixed?" Her head was low, and he persisted. "Billy Joe's got a decent job at the lumber mill."

"He don't know it yet," Lara said. "And you better not tell him, neither."

"You can't live in make-believe—hopin' it'll go away."

"There's a women's clinic over in Money. I can be in and back in two hours."

"Those are dangerous places," Ray protested. "It ain't like some dentist for a cleaning."

"And you ain't no expert all of a sudden, Ray." Lara looked at him sharply. "Maybe I best marry Billy Joe and get done with it."

Ray stopped walking and stood in the shadows. "You're only sixteen, Lara. Momma'd have a goat."

"Then we got us a new sibling. What of it?"

Ray shook his head firmly. "Best to tell Papa the truth." He sighed. "He's a practical-thinking man."

Lara plucked a few fallen branches up, snapped them, and bunched them in the leather carrier. She eyed her older brother and pointed at the upper tree leaves. "You see dollar bills growing on those limbs? Quick fixes cost money."

"And a baby can stifle your life forever, can't it?"

With the kindling filling her satchel, Lara turned and began striding back the way they'd come. "Papa wants to talk tonight. I suppose we go from there."

They walked single file through the woods and back across the yard to the farmhouse. Ray said, "He's stern most times, but he isn't stupid. And he loves us both."

Lara said nothing as they entered the backdoor off the kitchen.

May 29 – Saturday

The thick woods coursed along the backstretch of the two-story Middle School and sloped a quarter mile down toward the Tallahatchie River tributary. Unkempt soccer fields, a softball diamond, and a playground for younger kids with swings, monkey bars, and the like were on the grounds. On the adjacent lawn near the road stood the Community Baptist Church. Over where the woods started, a trio of picnic tables was perched near an old cobblestone wishing well.

Lara sat beside Billy Joe on one of the tables, facing the woods. They were discussing life in general and their own situation precisely. Frown lines creased Lara's young face. She was worried about her family and her father's advice from last night's talk. And concerned that Billy Joe, being older and more responsible, might not be taking their situation seriously enough.

Lara wore denim shorts and a green untucked shirt. Billy Joe was lean and rawboned, his face darkened by labor in the sun. His long-style hair curled at the tips. People said he was a good-looking boy from far away and even better close-up.

Lara said softly, "My Papa knows, Billy Joe. Momma hasn't said nothing, but Papa and Ray both know things for a fact."

"How could they? I didn't even know until three weeks ago."

"Well, I darn sure know, don't I?" She swiped a dark hair wisp from her forehead. "So's half the town by now. They can tell just by looking at me."

"BS." Billy Joe studied her hard. "You're the prettiest girl I know, Lara May. Whether you're sixteen or twenty-five, it don't matter to me."

"I'm in high school. I ain't old enough to become a mama."

"I told you I'd step up, didn't I?"

Lara rose and walked toward the trees but stopped and turned back. "I'm not ready to have babies, Billy Joe." The boy started to speak, but she cut him off. "And if'n I do, Papa will run us both out of town on the rail."

"That's crazy talk."

Lara shoved her hands in her front pockets. "What I'm telling you is Papa and me spoke last night. There was no debate back and forth. When he sets his mind to something—"

"His mind to what?"

"Setting up a quick fix." Lara crossed her arms. "We've got to scratch things back to zero between you and me. It'll be all right because Papa knows how medical fixes work. He's had to snip dogs and pigs before for gettin' feisty."

"What?" Billy Joe was incredulous. "That's dangerous, Lara. We both know it."

"It's the smartest option. That way, we get us a fresh start."

Billy Joe rose and faced her angrily. "You ain't fixing things with no coat hanger. That's downright a sin." He stepped forward and yelled at the thick trees. "No! No! No! It ain't right!"

Lara said calmly, "The lady Papa knows is an expert. He says Momma already went there maybe twice. Years back when he wanted more kids for fieldwork."

"You're not saying—"

"She convinced him we didn't have enough food for four mouths, let alone more of 'em."

Billy Joe was struck silent for a beat. Then: "Your Papa . . . In your heart, you know it isn't right, Lara."

"It's set up already. It's destiny."

Billy Joe strode away along the edge of the tree line and, this time, kept going. Turning back, he finally shouted, "It isn't destiny, Lara. It's called *murder*!"

With tears in her eyes, she watched him depart.

Saturday Night – 10:30 PM— Choctaw Ridge Forrest

The old wooden shack in the deep woods was dimly lit inside. A scarred metal barrel in the front yard glowed from within, casting a soft light around the area and creating pockets of deep shadows. Through the upper branches, a crescent moon peeked down between sailing clouds.

Papa parked the brown pickup truck along the narrow forest road, and they exited. He led the way toward the small cabin. Ray and Lara—wearing a shapeless gray sack dress—trailed behind. The slope-roofed house was barely visible amid the cluster of gnarled tree limbs on both sides.

Ray said, "I hope them sparks don't catch the brush."

"Old Hattie knows what she's doing by now."

The trio trudged forward through the clearing, arriving at last at the front door. Papa rapped twice, and it was answered by an eighty-eight-year-old lady who appeared twice that. She was a dark creole woman known for her midwife talents. Some locals praised her as a natural healer, while others called Old Hattie the "Witch of Choctaw Woods." She'd been around since Papa's grandfather had worked their farm.

Hattie had a hound dog who slept inside by the fire. Only his snores proved he wasn't a taxidermist's product. She motioned them to sit at her rickety dining table. As they did, she smiled warmly at Lara, who was pale, nervous, and close to shaking. In comfort, Hattie patted her head with a gentle hand and stroked away the hair strands from her forehead.

"You can calm yourself, sweetie. You're in the hands of our maker tonight."

Lara nodded, though desiring to flinch from the older woman's touch.

Papa said, "We're settled up, Hattie. Is there anything else you require?"

Hattie shook her head and set before them three tin cups. They were half-filled with the liquor she'd poured from a copper jug. The woman said, "Y'all sip my sweet rye. I brew it myself in the woods still. We'll get right down to the business at hand."

Papa sipped the homemade hootch from his cup, prompting his kids to follow. He remarked, "We wouldn't normally bring the boy along, but he's a friend of my daughter's beau."

Hattie nodded approval. She remained close behind Lara as if not planning to sit. "The drink settles your nerves. Not just the young'uns, but Papa too." She touched Lara's left shoulder. "Don't worry, young lady. This whole episode takes about twenty minutes. You'll leave here light as a baby robin."

Ray rolled his eyes, but Papa's stern look reminded him of his manners.

Hattie pulled a gray knitted shawl from the counter, draped it over Lara's shoulders, patted them, and said, "Drink up. We all need our nerve tonight." With a graceful smile, she finally sat down on Lara's right and held the girl's hand as if emphasizing her promise. Then, the older lady closed her eyes and lapsed into a mild trance. Her dry lips mumbled some vague prayer, and she whispered aloud, "Good. Very good," while nodding. After a bit, she blinked her eyes open. "We praise our Lord above. We will erase the past four months of your life, Miss Lara."

Ray and Papa watched nervously.

Hattie added, "You close your eyes and relax now, child. Let the warm numbness wash over you." Lara did as suggested, causing the elderly lady to smile. "Ahh, very good. Calm as a kitten." Finally, she released Lara's hand and told her to drink the last of her sweet rye.

Lara swallowed the dregs of her drink and slumped a bit in the chair.

To the men, Hattie said, "Same goes for y'all. We're in this here together, aren't we? Finish your drinks."

After they did, Hattie rose and set their cups in the small sink. She reached into her apron pocket, withdrew a small glass vial, and cautiously handed it to Papa. "Here's the other item you paid for. Be careful—it's ripe and ornery."

Papa slipped the object into his shirt pocket.

The elderly host then handed him a second item wrapped in an oilcloth. "Courtesy of old Doc Wanehouse," Hattie informed. "I bartered it for fresh porcupine quills." She winked at Ray like she'd revealed a secret. "Disposable kind. No need to return it."

Papa slid the three-inch gift into his pants pocket.

While this was happening, Lara had lapsed into a drowsy state from the potion and slumped her head to one arm across the table. Hattie informed the men it was time they left, and Papa and Ray moved toward the front door.

"You stir my fire outside. Leave the woman's work to us," Hattie said. "Should be fifteen minutes."

"That a promise?"

"Does a hound dog chase a coon?"

After they departed from the house, the matron turned to Lara. She helped the young girl up by one arm and guided her toward a back bedroom.

At the same time, outside by the fire drum, Ray asked, "You sure this is right, Papa?"

"Trust me. These old midwives know the tricks of feminine nature."

Satisfied, Ray employed a crusted black stick to stir the coals in the barrel. Sparks flared into the dry night air.

"Besides, I haven't steered you wrong before, have I?"

"No, sir."

While the two men stood beneath the leafy overhang and talked in somber tones, Lara lay on a narrow mattress in the compact bedroom inside the wooden shack. She was semi-conscious from the herbal tincture she'd been administered. She had her knees up and bare feet planted on the bed. Her dress was gathered around her waist, and her arms extended loosely at her sides.

Hattie laid her head on the girl's stomach and gently massaged her abdomen. She cooed, "That's good, sweetie. Just relax and breathe; relax and breathe." The elderly lady had placed a plastic covering over the bed quilt, and after a few minutes, a viscous fluid began to ooze out gently from between Lara's legs. The excretion soon turned clumpier with a darker, monthly-like substance that could have been a clot.

"The beauty of nature," Hattie whispered to the girl. "You done real good." The older female lifted her head and rose. She fetched a dark plastic bag and moved to the lower bed, sluicing the contents and fluid into the ten-inch bag with her weathered hands. She sealed it and set it aside on the nearby dresser top.

Hattie said calmly, "You can lower your legs, sweetie, and stand up. Be careful. It'll be shaky." After Lara stood, the older woman handed her dark towels and pointed to a large washtub in the room's corner. It contained three inches of fresh rainwater. Lara stepped in, used a soap bar to cleanse herself, then dried off with the towels.

Stepping out, she asked, "Is that it? I didn't feel much."

"It's the herb potion you drank," Hattie explained. "Your mind was eased. Your brother and Papa had regular rye, but I gave you the added potion that makes things flow. When you get home, you'll need the bathroom once or twice. And be sure you sleep wrapped with towels for dripping."

"Will I be sick? Or hurt tomorrow?"

"Uh-uh. All this is behind you now like you dreamed it, child."

She had moved close and helped Lara slip back into her bland frock and flat shoes. Hattie escorted the girl across the cabin's main room to the door. "You can work the fields tomorrow if you're up to it." The wise lady smiled. "Just a sad dream is all this is."

Lara hesitated at the door. "Miss Hattie, do you think I can have my baby? Little Billie? That was going to be her name. For a proper Christian burial in the woods?"

Hattie shook her head firmly. "Some things are best not lingered on. Been my experience. But you give it some thinking and pray in church tomorrow."

Lara nodded, understanding though disappointed. Her lips were pressed together.

"If you're still thinking that way, then come back to me Monday," Hattie whispered. "But it's over after that. Into dust, we shall return."

The elderly lady opened the door, and Lara slipped out into the night.

Sunday Evening – May 30 – Community Baptist Church

The summer twilight had turned dark. Nearly thirty people milled around outside the white clapboard church, nodding hellos, pausing to converse about this and that. A few young boys wore straw hats and thin ties, the girls in dresses. All wore their Sunday finest.

Light spilled out from inside the chapel, illuminating the steps and surrounding lawn. At the head of the walkway, Momma and Papa talked to Brother Taylor about his sermon on "Redemption." The dark preacher was thirty-three years old and possessed rawboned features.

Ten yards away, Ray was laughing with a freckle-faced former classmate, Becky Thompson. In the distance across the lawn from where they gossiped, Lara stood in a blue dress, cloaked shadows near the picnic tables. She was in an intense discussion with Billy Joe. Lara glanced back to the gathering at Ray, and their eyes met.

She turned back to Billy Joe, saying, "Done is done, Billy. We can return to our normal lives again."

Billy Joe replied tersely, "No, we can't, Lara. Your story don't sound right." He stepped one way before turning back to her. "And you don't look like you had no serious operation."

"I'm going back to Hattie tomorrow to... to reclaim little Billie."

"Back to the witch with her coat hanger?" He shook his head, frowning. "And who in God's name is Billie?"

"Your daughter, stupid. I already had her name picked out after you."

He shook his head and chewed his lower lip. "That's crazy, Lara. Plum crazy."

"Hattie's a kind lady, Billy Joe." She gazed back across at the church group, spotting Brother Taylor as he looked their way. "Besides,"—turning back to Billy Joe—"the Bible says respect our elders."

"And also respect new babies, too."

Lara's eyes narrowed. "We'll have ten more babies if'n you want." When he scowled, she added: "Just not while I ain't street legal."

"Newsflash, Lara." Billy Joe's face flushed. "You're not the first teen girl who ever got pregnant."

Before she could respond, he added, "Tell your Papa we'll make him ten little farmhands 'tween us. Maybe he'll accept me then."

"Or maybe he'll shotgun ya first."

With a head shake, Billy Joe stomped away along the trees. Over his shoulder, he called: "And stay away from that old witch, or I'll report you to Sheriff Carver."

Lara watched him enter his pickup parked in the street shadows. He sped away into the dark evening, not bothering to flick on the headlights.

Over near the church steps, Brother Taylor and Papa watched the young couple's drama from afar. Brother Taylor remarked, "Billy Joe's driving off lightless."

Papa said, "That boy never possessed one lick of sense."

Monday – May 31 – Choctaw Ridge Forest

Lara wore her bibs with a t-shirt underneath. The sun stretched from a morning yawn and lifted against the tear-blue sky. Birds chased one another amid the dense branches, and squirrels chittered as she stepped across the clearing and rapped on Hattie's cottage door. The elderly lady answered unsurprised and handed Lara a burlap pouch containing the sealed, dark plastic bag.

Hattie said, "You and the Lord do what need be."

Lara nodded and accepted the satchel silently.

"Mind yourself now, sweetie," the midwife advised. "You swallow five black currents and suck a pine needle before you roll with that boy again, you hear?"

Lara nodded and departed. Behind her, Hattie gave a sharp whistle and closed the door after her hound had limped inside.

In Lara's small bedroom that night, beneath the fingernail moon and breeze tickling the ghostly window curtains, she curled beneath her bedcovers. After ten minutes of being unable to drift asleep, Lara began to hum: "*Just another sleepy Choctaw day....*"

She had the satchel tucked beneath one arm. She closed her eyes again and whispered, "Goodnight, little Billie. Sleep safe."

Tuesday – June 1 – Tallahatchie Bridge – Noon

Billy Joe and Lara walked solemnly along the wooden bridge's planks toward the center. Both wore their work clothes. Billy Joe pulled a sandwich from his dungaree pocket and frowned at it. He flung it disgustedly over the wooden bridge rail and didn't watch as it dropped into the brown current below.

Lara glanced back at him, and he said, "I've got no appetite."

"This here's a religious ceremony anyways."

"Sacrilegious. More like."

"It's got to be done, Billy Joe," Lara insisted. "For us getting on with our lives. And the baby–"

"Ain't no baby. You killed our baby."

"Nonsense. I met a nice lady living in the woods and shared a cup of rye. That's all there's to it."

"Witch's brew." He scowled at Lara, dragging two steps behind. "And maybe there's more to it. Maybe y'all danced naked around some blazing firepit."

She shook her head in silence—no point arguing.

They paused at the bridge's center with Lara holding the pouch. Billy Joe remained two yards back. He stared off at the opposite bank, not watching her, looking beyond the thick trees at nothing.

Lara announced solemnly: "Dear Lord. We're all only human, and we all make mistakes. So please, Lord, accept the soul of our Billie into Limbo with all the other tiny babies there—"

"Who ain't ever lived to see a sunrise."

Lara ignored him. She separated the dark plastic bag from inside the burlap pouch and dumped the viscous contents into the river below. She also released the bag and pouch and watched as they spun and fluttered in the breeze before floating swiftly downstream.

Billy Joe stepped back onto the bridge and bent at the waist with his fists balled; then, he moved back to the railing and shrieked angrily down at the muddy river. Turning, he glared at Lara, who continued gazing at the water below.

"In the name of bloody Jesus," Billy Joe shouted at the sky. "I didn't just witness that."

Lara reached inside her upper bib pocket and tossed a handful of violets into the river. She turned and faced him. "It's in the Lord's hands now."

Billy Joe's eyes narrowed. "We commend thy spirit, right? Simple as dumped pudding."

"We'll have a dozen babies after we're married—like we talked."

Billy Joe turned and stomped away down the bridge's center, rattling the planks, not caring if any vehicles came. Lara watched him angle off the edge and disappear inside the thick bushes and trees cluster. She glanced across the opposite bank and spotted a hiker inside the tree line. He turned and vanished into the woods, and Lara could swear he looked like Brother Taylor from the church. It mattered little. She reached into another pocket and tossed violets below before ambling in the opposite direction that Billy Joe had departed.

Wednesday – June 2 – Lumber Mill

Papa's pickup truck pulled in and stopped in the dusty gravel parking lot of the lumber mill. It was after five p.m., and the employees' lot was emptying. A handful of men sat in the shade of an overhang, conversing, their empty lunch buckets beside them. Ray whistled out the window at Billy Joe, who stood near the men with an open canteen in his hand.

Billy Joe waved at Ray, handed another friend the canteen, and sauntered toward the idling pickup. "If it ain't old Coody," Billy Joe called as he approached.

"Hey, McAllister. We were in the area buying pallets. You need a lift somewhere?"

Billy Joe eyed the stack of pallets in the pickup's back. His gaze caught Lara's papa, whose creased eyes possessed their usual dangerous look. However, Billy

Joe already considered himself part of his future family. Only a matter of time. He said, "I usually hike the half-mile to my place. But why not? It's steamy as a swamp out here."

Ray opened the passenger door and scootched over as Billy Joe climbed inside, saying, "Much obliged. I live up the ridge along the old Moose Road."

Ray said he remembered Lara telling them.

Papa roared a half-circle around the lot, the rear tires spitting gravel dirt. Ray said to Billy Joe: "I seen you and my sis having words last Sunday." He grinned evenly. "I suppose outside the church is a decent place to argue and all."

Billy Joe laughed. "You know women. When the blood rises in their necks, it's best to hightail it and let things cool a bit."

Even Papa smiled. "You know she's a teenager? Our Lara?" His eyes stayed on the road.

Yessir. I sure do. Ray here and me been friends since way back. So I respect your daughter like I do my own mama."

Papa snorted, watching the heavy trees sweep past on both sides.

"It ain't about respect," Ray said knowingly. "Heck, Billy Joe, we're both twenty-two. I know Lara's cute and all, but there's lots of fish swimming in the river."

Billy Joe glanced their way. "I shouldn't take a shine to Lara? Is that what I'm hearing?"

Papa cruised past the turnoff for Billy Joe's place up the ridge and continued another half-mile down to the crossroads leading to the Tallahatchie Bridge.

"Sorry, sir," Billy Joe said at last. "I wasn't watching. My turn was back by the birch pond. I can get out here and hike it back."

Papa instead swung south and drove a brief distance to a four-way stop short of the railroad tracks. He paused with the engine running, glancing across at Billy Joe. He said, "Let's park 'er up near the bridge and take a walk, Billy Joe. A man-to-man would do us both some positive."

Billy Joe stared at the older man's snake eyes. He remained angry at what had transpired two days before with Lara and what she'd done throwing that *stuff* off the bridge. He figured her daddy was right: clearing the air between them wouldn't be the worst thing in the world. After all, it's what families do.

"Fair enough, sir," Billy Joe agreed, watching as they neared the Tallahatchie Bridge.

Papa drove forward and cleared the train tracks, angling the pickup to a halt on the roadside short of the bridge's drive-up. He hopped from the truck and strode onto the grassy slope above the flowing river below them. He stared out at the mud-colored waters swirling around the heavy wooden pylons.

Billy Joe looked through the open window at the afternoon sun, watching the breeze sway the upper tree branches around them. He felt Ray studying him and shrugged with mild indifference.

Ray said, "Talking to Papa would be right smart, Billy Joe. Clear some air. Besides, we've come this far, haven't we?"

Billy Joe nodded and exited the passenger door. Ray followed him, slamming the truck door as he hopped out. They approached the wiry older man who stood on the weedy river slope with his back to them.

"If I did something to upset you, sir, I apologize," Billy Joe said humbly. "If I deserve a good tongue lashing, I'll take it like a grown-up. But just so you know, I care mightily for your daughter." He glanced at Ray just behind him. "And to you, Ray. You know I treat Lara with gentlemanly respect."

Casting a sidelong glance, Papa strode past the low brush and up the mild incline onto the creaky old two-lane bridge. Billy Joe shrugged at Ray, and together, they followed Papa.

Ray asked Billy as they walked: "What's crazy Stanley Miller up to these days?"

"Quit his job at the sawmill," Billy replied, reaching the point where the bridge incline leveled off. "They say he's moving to Jackson for the steel plant there."

"Better taverns in Jackson," Ray conceded. "He'll fit right in. How about Shorty Ebli?"

"Joined the Army last spring. Passed basic training after his butt shrunk two sizes." Both men laughed. "Hard picturing him in a uniform, though."

"Like those old Army photos of Elvis," Ray added. "Back when he first got drafted."

They chuckled together while progressing along the edge of the traffic-less bridge. The wooden beams crisscrossed above them, stretching to the center's arching crown.

An approaching train whistle blew unseen through the dense trees a quarter mile back along the river. The clatter of tracks drowned away the sound for the next five minutes. There'd be no traffic, though there seldom was on the remote bridge since the dam upstream was under repair. Papa stopped at the bridge rail and watched the eddies swirl around the wooden pylons below. He turned at the younger men's approach.

"No offense, Billy Joe," Papa announced, "but I think you should vacate these parts. Maybe find another city across the state to call your home."

Billy Joe was taken aback at the suggestion. "No offense yourself, sir. But I like Choctaw Ridge. Born, raised, and got kin around." He frowned at Papa. "Besides, I found the girl I cherish. I want to settle down with Lara as soon as she's old enough."

Ray said, "You can find another Lara on any Tupelo street corner."

Billy Joe studied him, gauging his seriousness.

"And suppose I don't permit such a union with my daughter?" Papa said tersely. "You got yourself a reputation around these parts as a slacker so and so."

Billy Joe puffed his chest. "I sewed some wild oats after turning eighteen. Just ask Ray—we did what all fellas do. Nothing half bad." His face flushed, and his fists balled. "So, no offense to your words, but shouldn't your daughter decide herself about her future?"

"Now, Billy Joe," Ray protested. "Don't go getting half-cocked—"

"Isn't that what Brother Taylor preaches?" Billy Joe's eyes searched them both. "A woman's got her final say in who she chooses—like the Bible says."

"From what I gather, son, you and the Good Book aren't exactly on a first-name basis."

"True enough, sir. But that don't mean a leopard's spots can't change." Billy Joe's tone was challenging. "I'd even be a decent farmer if'n my mind was in it."

"Fat chance," Papa huffed.

The older man stepped further to the bridge's center. They had the structure to themselves. Not the barest glimmer of a vehicle all this time. Below them, the river waters continued to churn downstream.

"Lara's captured my heart, sir. I'll kindly admit it." Billy Joe trailed Papa by two steps. "We can't wait to start our own family."

Papa stopped and peered over the wooden rail at the moving current below. "Ray. How deep do you think it is down there?"

"They say thirty feet, dead center." Ray remained behind them both on the roadway. "Deep enough for a man to drown, anyhow."

Billy Joe stepped up to the rail and studied the brown river below. While doing so, Ray lurched up and grabbed him from behind in a tight bear hug. Surprised, Billy Joe struggled against his friend's biceps and forearms. Both young men were lean and hard from hoisting logs and hay bales all their lives.

Struggling backward, Billy Joe shouted, "Ray! What are you—"

From behind them, Papa called, "Hold him tight, son." Withdrawing a syringe from his shirt pocket, Papa injected the sharp needle through the cloth of Billy Joe's shirt. The point pierced the back flesh of his bicep as the depressed plunger emptied.

Billy Joe screamed, "What the hell are you—"

"It's biblical, son," proclaimed Papa, withdrawing the needle. "Eye for an eye." He stepped away in long strides toward the bridge's middle.

Ray spun and released Billy Joe seconds later, backing himself ten yards away. Near the wooden railing, Billy Joe grabbed his upper arm in shock. The surprise attack had come so suddenly that his anger hadn't yet taken hold. Positioned between his attackers, he stared at the hypodermic needle still in Papa's hand. "What did you do?" He shouted, swinging his eyes from father to son. "What did you do?"

"Protecting my sister," answered Ray bitterly. "It's old Hattie's timber-rattler venom. Ain't no man survived it even once."

Billy Joe glared at them with bulging eyes. Still gripping his upper arm, he staggered forward before falling to his knees near the bridge's edge. After a minute of moaning, he rolled onto his back near the railing. His body tremored, and sweat glistened across his forehead and ruddy cheeks. He gasped aloud: "Help me, for God's sake." He closed his eyes and curled in pain; his teeth gritted behind twisted lips. "Call the rescue...."

Papa moved closer and nudged the man with the toe of his work boot.

Ray whispered, "What now? If a car comes along—"

Papa's eyes swept both sides of the empty bridge. A second freight train had whistled distantly during the attack, but now even the tree birds were eerily silent.

Ray looked at his father, and Papa nodded toward the rail and the flowing water below. "Shouldn't we weight him?" the boy asked.

"Uh-uh. Venom swells the lungs," Papa said knowingly. "River'll take care of the rest."

June 3 – Thursday

After a full day's work in the hot fields, the battered, dusty pickup cruised up the driveway, scattering the chickens, and parked outside the farmhouse as suppertime approached. Ray and Lara trailed Papa to the back door, where they wiped their feet on the mat before entering.

While they took turns washing up, Momma called from the kitchen that Brother Taylor had stopped by earlier and left them a copy of the *Choctaw Sun-Times*.

"What did he want?" asked Ray, entering the kitchen while toweling his hands dry.

"Said he might stop by next Sunday for dinner." After a pause, she added, "Also, there's a death listed in the paper he says we might want to know about."

Papa grunted. "He say who?"

"Uh-uh. And I didn't want to read any sad news and spoil my appetite."

Lara entered the kitchen and helped Momma place the food bowls on the table. After they were seated, with Popa saying grace, they crossed themselves before commencing to scoop food onto their plates. Ray, however, was distracted. He asked, "Where's that paper? They've got the results of the Tilson's heifer auction."

"On the counter there." Lara reached for the paper and handed it to her brother.

Ray flipped open a page, but Momma quickly wrested it from him and set it back on the counter. "We ain't heathens. The news can wait till after we eat."

Papa spoke up. "I'd like to know who's important enough for Brother Taylor to advise us knowing."

Ray fetched the newspaper back and flipped it open, ignoring his mother's scowl.

"Let your sister read it, son," Papa commanded. Ray frowned and handed the paper to Lara. Momma continued scowling at them all.

Ignoring the national headlines, Lara opened to the local news section, and her eyes scanned. A moment later, she gasped audibly, her mouth wide in disbelief.

"What is it?" demanded Ray.

The *Choctaw Sun-Times* ran the story on the third page beneath a small header an inch below the fold. The undersized headline was listed under the news banner: **LOCAL MAN'S BODY FOUND.**

(Lara's voice) Reading aloud, her voice quavering as she progressed:

"The body of William Joseph McAllister, 23, of Choctaw Ridge, was discovered last evening by two mudcat fishermen working from a small barge in the Tallahatchie River. McAllister was a Choctaw Ridge resident who worked as a local logger at the Montague Sawmill Company. County Sheriff's Deputies on the scene summoned the Choctaw County coroner, Dr. Miles Lamar, who arrived shortly after that and confirmed the remains as those of Mr. McAllister. The Cause of Death was recorded as "Deceased by drowning."

Lara flung the newspaper aside, eliciting a gasp from Momma. They watched silently as her face flushed and tears coursed down her cheeks. Before anyone spoke, she rose, slapped the napkin on her plate, then exited the kitchen while sobbing hysterically. She rushed off toward her bedroom.

Rising from her chair, Momma called loudly: "Lara, honey. We know how much you . . ." Her voice trailed off.

"Should I go make sure she's okay?" Ray offered, eyeing them both.

Shaking her head, Momma said, "No. We all stay put. She just needs to cry herself out, is all. Nothing any of us can say will help none."

Papa said, "Read the rest, boy."

(Ray's voice) reading aloud:

"The victim was unmarried and leaves behind his mother, Risa, his father, Woodrow, and one younger brother, Thomas, age 19. The Porseau-Waller Funeral Parlor is managing the arrangements. Details will follow after the proper formalities have been finalized.

The Choctaw County Sheriff's Department deputies have confirmed through family members and coworkers that McAllister had suffered from recent bouts of depression and non-work-related stress. Possible suicide off the old Tallahatchie Bridge has not yet been ruled out as contributing to his unfortunate demise. However, Sheriff's Deputy Roland Morse further vaguely suggested: "When the apple barrel smells sour, you've likely got yourself a rotten one inside."

"What the blazes does that mean?" Papa asked, squinting his eyes at them.

Momma said sternly, "Mind your tongue. We're at the table."

"I guess that he had some sort of sickness, maybe?" Ray offered, shrugging.

Papa said, "That boy never did have a lick of sense." They all silently continued with their meal. "Mind passing me those biscuits, Momma?"

She did as requested, passing the biscuit plate as Ray continued reading aloud.

(Ray's voice):

"Services will be held at Choctaw Community Baptist Church. Further notification will be provided when the proper times are decided. From the offices of *The Choctaw Sun-Times*, we express our deepest condolences to the friends and family members of William Joseph (Billy Joe) McCallister. May he rest in peace with the Lord Almighty."

Three rooms away, Lara couldn't stop crying while lying wrapped in her quilt in her bedroom. Fifteen long minutes later, she swiped the tears from her eyes with the back of her hand. Reaching beneath her pillow for her diary, she scrawled in pen:

They tell me Billy Joe McCallister's jumped off the Tallahatchie Bridge.

With her tears splashing the paper, she tucked the diary beneath her pillow and continued sobbing again.

Author's Note:

The above story is a work of Interpretive Fiction. It conveys a pre-story involving the characters that appeared in the 1967 song composed and performed by artist Bobbie Gentry. The original song and lyrics of "Ode to Billie Joe" can be found on multiple free online song sites. They cannot be included here due to legal copyright protections.

For the sake of clarity and preference, the author has chosen to alter the story's male protagonist to the masculine name "Billy Joe," rather than the song's published title of "Billie Joe"—which rumors persist was mislabeled as a typographical error from song's original title. No clarification of the title's alteration has been conceded by either the artist herself or any label spokesperson.

Decades have passed since the song's debut, and thousands of listeners, theorists, and fans still debate the haunting refrains of "Ode to Billie Joe." They will likely also argue about *The Mystery of Choctaw Ridge*—the same way debates continue over Agatha Christie whodunnits—where differing theories about what occurred on that June 3rd day on Choctaw Ridge abound. Lively discussions about what might have been thrown off the Tallahatchie Bridge into the muddy waters below. And why might the distraught Billy Joe McCallister have leaped off the bridge to his death? Why was the family's dinner discussion over the young man's suicide so seemingly casual? Why was it reported that the family's young daughter had been spotted earlier on the bridge with Billy Joe, throwing something unknown off the bridge? And why—at the song's end—does she confess returning to the "suicide" bridge and tossing flowers into the murky waters below? Sin? Remorse? Guilt? Perhaps all of the above?

Most importantly, like "Ode to Billie Joe" itself, will we ever learn the answers to these complex questions?

The song lyrics can be searched on numerous online platforms and music sites.

Writer/s: Bobbie Gentry

Publisher: Spirit Music Group

Lyrics licensed and provided online by *LyricFind*

Final Note:

The above story does not claim that the events reconstructed in the fictional account *The Mystery of Choctaw Ridge* are factual. Like the song, we will leave that debate to the amateur sleuths and our erstwhile readers.

Almost Died Event # 2 – BURN OR DROWN – age 12

Age twelve and living in Green Bay. Three of my friends were Boy Scouts. They convinced me to join the troop so we could attend the weekend jamboree together. One week later, we drove to Camp Bear Paw. I was not a good camper and couldn't sleep. We sneaked around the lake the next day and played mumblety-peg with a jackknife, then lit leaves piles with stick matches and cigarette lighters. Lighter fluid splashed on my sock, and my foot lit up in flames. I jumped into the nearby lake. It was eight feet deep. I tried to push off the bottom weed bed, and my ankles were stuck in the muck. My guardian angel told me to turn them sideways, and somehow that worked. I floated up to the surface seconds before I would've drowned.

FATHERLY JUSTICE

Logline: When a rural farming couple discovers their ten-year-old daughter has vanished into the adjacent forest, they must pull out all the stops before she disappears forever.

Willow's lunch was finished. Her mom preferred to handwash the dishes, and Willow usually helped dry them. Afterward, she was allowed to play outside for a half-hour. It aided digestion, mom said. Exercise and fresh air cleared the girl's head for another three hours of afternoon home studies.

Today, with the sky clouding up, mom sent her outside before the raindrops began to fall. The family lived by Mother Nature's clock. The cows and her dad had their daily appointments in the barn. The chickens did what chickens do all day. The dogs understood to the second when their food bowls would magically appear on the back porch. Even Rufus, the rooster, hollered at the first scarlet hint of daybreak.

Clockwork.

The wind was picking up, Willow noted. The sheets ghost-flapped on the lines, and the three-foot-tall calf door on the barn was clapping. At least when the breeze kicked up her dancing heels. She was already outside with Clay, so her mom had no concerns. The dog's job was to look after her. The chocolate lab was well-suited to the task with his ready muzzle, muscular shoulders, and haunches.

Willow lazed her way past the hen house and beyond the edge of the conifer bushes. She fired a yellow rubber ball off into the woods. Clay rushed after it and returned it a minute later. He smiled his lopsided grin and dropped it near her purple tennis shoes.

"Good boy," Willow said, smiling. She grabbed the ball, and he looked up at her with mocha eyes that would melt the heart of a princess.

Rufus cackled from the edge of the rust-colored shed. He strutted three steps one way before turning back like a dedicated private patrolling his turf.

"Thirty minutes," her mom (Lita) called from the porch. "Not a minute more."

Willow nodded. It was getting windier, and she was glad she had grabbed her light jacket. The screen door banged as her mother disappeared back inside. Staring at her best friend, Willow said, "At least we got out of drying dishes."

Clay whined, ready for another ball pitch. She crossed him up and fired it behind the barn, opposite the woods. The dog bounded after the rolling object.

Willow could hear her dad's tractor a quarter mile off, bouncing over the soybean field. He wore headphones, she knew, listening to Z-Z Top or Lynyrd Skynyrd or another of his oldies bands. She preferred modern songs flavored with a salsa beat. She liked melody better than lyrics but still had a soft spot for songs that told a story. Mostly about boys who left you, then realized they screwed up. Or about messy romances between friends like in *Twilight*.

Sometimes, a rhythm got stuck in her head, so Willow allowed it to continue on repeat play. But this only happened at times when she felt lonely. Which was often, it seemed, because there was almost too much silence and solitude amid the trees and hills and farm fields. Especially at night when the frogs and crickets played their two-note serenade. Not much story going on in their racket.

She watched now as Clay got distracted behind the barn. It might be a gopher. He dropped the ball, sniffed a few steps, and did the same in a different direction.

"Bring it back, Clay," Willow encouraged. "Don't be a putz!"

It was a word her friend Marcy used in bible study. But not when Pastor Roy's wife was around. Willow had tried it out a few times on her own and liked the way it sounded. But she only used it on Clay because it sounded funny. Maybe it hit home. The dog forgot about the gopher and trotted back toward her with the ball in his teeth, stopping a few yards short.

"C'mon, boy. Bring it here."

One of her dad's oldies popped into her head. She hummed to get the pitch right and sang out, "Rollin, rollin, rollin, keep them doggies rollin . . . *Rawhide!*" She made a whip-crack sound while snapping her wrist. Willow laughed when Clay cocked his head as if saying to her, "You're sure weird!"

He dropped the ball at her foot, nudging her ankle. She plucked it up, ignoring the drool.

Willow decided it was an excellent time to visit the stream—her favorite place on Earth and only a minute into the woods. The tree glade stretched about forty yards sideways before it thinned into tall patches of weeds, which led to the next road past. The stream ran lengthwise up through the center of the mile-long strip of forest. The water was about two feet deep, cruising over smooth rocks and stuck logs and branches Mother Nature put there when she felt like it. It was a pleasant moving stream. It gurgled in the spring, especially after the snowmelt.

Across the creek, a fifteen-minute tromp through the denser woods led to a clearing where the spooky old hay barn stood. It was a thicker forest, and Willow visited it sometimes. But don't tell mom because she didn't like her wandering past where the chicken coop stood. It would be peaceful in the run-down barn. Free from the wind shaping the clouds into dark battleships and shielding off the sun.

Looking up, Willow saw the high branches doing the same hula dance she'd done in her second-grade play. She was littler then and not being home-schooled. She was ten now—ready for modern dances—maybe with boys and stuff. Leave the hula dancing to the smaller kids.

Willow tossed the yellow rubber ball (with the green "G" stamp) deep into the trees again. Clay's hindquarters disappeared after it. She followed in a slow walk, knowing he'd get distracted by smells and such. She stepped around a moldy stump and some elderberry bushes. The air smelled loamy from damp leaves and underbrush.

It was a netherworld of dark shadows and gray light. Willow slipped further beneath the tree cover. Peaceful and serene. The trill of a jaybird called, and above, she pictured a dozen fat crows looking down at her with jet-black eyes.

Even in the woods where she stood, she could still discern the groan of her dad's tractor in the far-off fields. Willow realized she couldn't see Clay anywhere. Nor could she hear him clumping through the bushes. He'd likely found something more interesting to sniff at, maybe through the tree clearing by the brook.

Willow spotted the yellow ball in a cluster of ferns. She was about to pick it up but stopped. A man stood fifteen yards away, leaning casually against a white birch. She recognized his straw-colored hair and froze. She'd seen him in the forest a few times before, staring out at her but never speaking. Then he disappeared like a magician.

But not this time. His smile was disconcerting now, and something about him warned of danger. Worse than that, he held her missing green ball—with the yellow "G" stamp. The one she'd lost here weeks ago.

"Hello, Willow," the man said. "I found your other ball." He flipped and caught it.

A hundred thoughts rushed through her head. She managed to stutter, "Where's my dog?" She looked past him, eyes swinging this way and that opposite the stream. "Where's Clay?"

"Maybe he went home."

"Clay!" Willow shouted, looking all around. The thick vegetation swallowed her voice. "Here, boy!" She whistled twice.

Only the wind's *swish* sounded through the high branches, accompanied by the far-off chitter of tree birds and the thirsty gurgle of the nearby stream.

"Clay!" Now more urgently.

The sun stayed hidden behind the clouds. The silent woods closed around them, and still, the dog did not answer her desperate calls.

"I know we said ten G's," Cory Mowry said into his phone. "But it's twenty now." He listened. "Cuz she's special—that's why. She'll increase your twenty a hundredfold."

Pausing, he added, "I'm sending pics to you. Three good ones."

He waited a minute, listening as the leader of the trafficking ring in Minneapolis spoke in his ear. Mowry said, "Yeah. Figured you'd agree." He glanced around the room. "Profit margin, right—payout's well beyond the cost?" He listened again before confirming: "Twenty G's, then. Ten p.m. The usual place."

The sex trafficker voiced another comment, to which Mowry replied, "I know, right? But she *swears* she's only ten."

After ending the connection, he stared out the door and studied the room's open door across the hallway. The girl remained bound to the wooden chair. Mowry heard the dog's low whines and whimpers and glanced at his 9mm in case the canine came charging at him with teeth bared. Instead, the mutt was just now coming around. It grunted, wheezing as if clearing its head of cobwebs.

The animal turned and spotted him. It whined again. The young girl's head lolled, coming around as well. She mumbled into the duct tape across her mouth. Never once had she glanced his way during his phone talk. At least she was alive. He'd been concerned about her raspy breathing earlier, worried that he'd doped her too strong for her slender body weight.

Mowry stepped out into the hallway and closed their room door, separating them and clicking the lock. The warehouse was large and unoccupied. It had taken only remedial lockpicking skills for him to enter and set up his drug shop. The prior occupants had even left the electricity running. Sweet.

Back in his room again, he opened the refrigerator and withdrew a plastic container. He laid a paper towel on the counter, grabbed a clump of raw ground beef from the container, and plopped it down.

On the long table behind him, Mowry grabbed the small plastic baggie. He crumbled a few powdered sedative flakes onto the meat and used his knife to mash it all together.

The Ross farmhouse. Thankfully, the rain had held off. Lita removed her garden kickers and slipped into sneakers. Her canvas bag contained beets and radishes, and she rinsed them under running water at the sink.

She noticed the stove clock read 2 p.m. Willow was not in her usual spot at the dining room table. Her daughter was supposed to be doing math or physics problems today—Lita couldn't remember which—and the grandfather clock's stern ticking caused her to beckon:

"Willow? You in the bathroom?"

Silence as the clock chimed twice.

Lita dried her hands and drifted from one room to the next. She peeked into the den and the bathroom before climbing the stairs to the second floor. Her daughter's bed was made, the room modestly cleaned. Khaki shorts on the bedspread. Stuffed dolls, boy-band posters, Jesus on the cross. They all stared at her from the chairs and walls.

Downstairs again, she grabbed her mobile phone and studied it. Nothing. She slipped out the back porch door and surveyed the yard, the barn, and the storage sheds. Lita searched both sides of the house on the move, then peered out past the henhouse with mounting concern. She studied the usual spot where her daughter and Clay entered the woods when exploring.

She whistled three times—a signal. Seconds later, old Satchmo hobbled from the barn where he'd been dozing with the cows. Lita turned a half-circle, and her voice lifted:

"Willow! Come on, sweetie." Even louder: "Get back in the house right now."

A blackbird answered from somewhere. Lita distinguished Bram's tractor grinding far off in the field but couldn't see him around the barn's edge. The sky showed darker clouds forming in the north, and the first plops of rain splashed her forearm. Bram would cut things short and head in if the drops continued.

They had a system between them where his phone lit up for messages. Lita texted with her thumbs: *Seen Willow? Not in the house.*

Her phone buzzed back: Not since before. Coming in. Rain.

She walked across the yard, flung open the barn and shed doors, and called inside. No answer. She advanced opposite past the henhouse, shushing the cluckers and Rufus as he strutted about trying to impress her. Lita entered the woods between a pair of birch trees, stepping over the bramble and underbrush.

She gave a crisp whistle.

"Willow? Clay?" Her voice echoed off the moss and ferns and was swallowed by the sway of high tree branches. No answer. Not far away, she could hear the soft babble of the flowing creek. A squirrel scampered somewhere. A woodpecker knocked a hollow sound.

Everything was calm and silent. The rain was yet too soft to penetrate the leafy canopy.

The humming night air made the forest feel swollen. It was almost nine p.m. now, Willow guessed. She wished she had her mom's phone. Any phone. Even earbuds. Anything to block the stupid guy's yakking on and on. She still had a headache from the sleep stuff he must've slipped into her sandwich, which didn't help matters.

At least Willow knew where they were now. There was no mistaking the creepy old, deserted barn in the woods. It was perched across the stream, about eighty yards from where their farmhouse stood. The older kids had named the place "haunted," and the idea had stuck. Willow didn't know if ghosts were real or just something the movies made up. But the place sure seemed spooky enough, either day or night, especially with the moon's pale glow, the witch-finger trees, hooting owls, and mysterious scuffling sounds. Besides all this, and despite a half-dozen visits to the barn in the past, Willow avoided climbing up into the rotting hayloft once inside. Especially after reading how brown recluse spiders liked to nest in barn lofts.

This time, however, was different. They were up in the scary hayloft now. The guy kept on blabbering like he was on speed pills or something. Anyone a quarter mile off could likely hear him. Willow hoped so. Someone listening who might give a "shout out." Then she'd kick the guy in his shin and run for it. Except she couldn't—not with Clay being hurt and cord-tied to a rotting roof beam.

She patted her dog's head now where they sat and hugged his neck. He looked up with sad eyes, and his body shivered. Clay's hip was injured. Her parents needed to get him to the vet for a shot. But until that could happen, it was up to Willow to make sure they both survived until morning. Her dad always reminded her she had to become a "leader."

At least the rain had stopped for a bit. Yet it didn't prevent the man from blabbing on his phone like a teenage girl. Or, when he wasn't, to chatter at her like he was making a speech at the summer fair. Other times, his calls lasted only a minute. To Willow, he claimed to be an "entrepreneur." Or something of the sort. He predicted he'd be wealthy and famous in only a year or two. Have a yacht boat and a show on TV. Without smiling, he had added:

"If our chips fall lucky red, right?"

Willow blinked and looked away.

~

Bram and Lita had searched for hours until dusk descended, and the shadows filled in. Nightfall now, and they were back at the house. Neither would surrender hope. Of course, they had summoned the county sheriff but learned that only two patrol units were available due to funding cuts by the County Board. Two deputies had visited the house and taken their statements. Lita provided photos of Willow, one hugging Clay, taken last spring. The apologetic deputies had driven off after advising the couple that their best bet was to keep their phones handy and stay put in case the girl called or returned home.

After they'd departed, Bram and Lita shared looks of disbelief. They needed to stay calm despite their anger and frustration. Together, they would react the same as any parents: they'd search for their daughter on their own.

The politicians be damned.

Besides, they knew the woods well enough and their daughter's habits. Their search party would consist of them alone. Bram told her he refused to sit around waiting for their phone to ring, a stranger's voice saying, "Please take a seat, ma'am." Or "I'm afraid we have bad news, sir."

With limited options, they would formulate a plan and search for themselves.

They wolfed down small sandwiches and discussed a plan of attack. Knowing Willow's habits, they decided Clay was likely with her. They would separate to cover more ground, staying connected via their mobile phones. Lita would drive the pickup north along the familiar country stretches. She'd shine the roads for signs across a three-mile area. Explore the railroad tracks. Rap on every farmhouse door in the county if necessary.

Bram would work the lower wooded grounds—take a second look opposite the stream again. They had already combed through the dense forest, shouting Willow and Clay's name fifty times. They'd sifted through the unkempt weeds surrounding the old hay barn and even checked inside the creepy place. Nothing but spiders, rodent droppings, and rainwater seeping in through the worm-eaten rafters.

The barn was an unholy eyesore. Weekend partiers had left pot bongs, tin foil, junky furniture, and upended wooden crates, all scarred by melted candles and cigarette burns. There was a sagging couch, discarded food wrappers, used condoms, shattered booze, and empty beer bottles. Slapping the word pigsty on the place would offend even the laziest old sow.

The inky night created layers of silent shadows. Bram decided the odds had already shifted, and not for the better. He also understood time was growing thin.

Something awful must have happened. But what kind of something? Willow was too sensible to venture carelessly into the woods, which left an accident or a head-to-rock tumbling injury. Something traumatic. Otherwise, if it were some garden variety accident, Bram guessed they'd have heard something by now. The variety of grim possibilities wrenched his guts.

Not knowing was worse than whatever outcome awaited.

He moved silently through the dense shadows, working the puzzle in his head, scanning side to side with his flash beam. A ten-year-old and her dog were missing. Nothing positive ever came from that story premise. On the plus side, Willow might be young, but she was bright and clever. She'd use the "country smarts" she'd been blessed with.

Stepping through weeds and spongy underbrush, Bram carried his companion of choice: a dark iron crowbar. He'd been taught never to enter the woods unarmed at half Willow's age. A bear, wolf, snake, or any rabid animal could attack with deadly force. It's how they were made—nothing personal. As things stood, however, Bram wouldn't mind having his double barrel along, but he could cover ground faster this way. The heavy steel bar was his preference.

Moving with purpose, he soon discerned the outline of the old, haunted barn. Bram extinguished his flashlight. When faced with uncertainty, it was better not to reveal your position.

He paused behind a tall ash tree, studying the decrepit barn in the vague moonlight. The weed-strewn place lurked like a giant tumor among the murky trees. The dampness helped conceal his presence, allowing him to watch and listen unseen. At first, the sound came quietly, a scratchy far-off tone, fluttering through the night as if coming from an old-time radio.

Bram notched his head to listen better. Then he had it: the tone sounded like the monologue speech of a lonesome drunk. Or, even more likely, a one-way telephone discussion.

Keeping his ears perked another few seconds, he decided he was correct.

Bram proceeded cautiously forward another ten yards, picturing from earlier how the right barndoor was stuck permanently half-open. It was almost pitch-black inside, the barest glimmer of light showing between the rotting sideboards. Its glow was as faint as a firefly if it was a phone. Bram also recalled the open doors of the upper hay drop, situated around the barn's far side. They appeared like a dark cycloptic eye staring out into the open forest. But he knew the flat surface was too high to scale, so he erased the idea.

A glance at his phone reported 9:20 p.m. The darkness remained pressing, with the moon and stars hidden behind murky clouds.

An owl hooted. Rainwater dripped from the upper leaves. The surrounding lavender bushes emitted a pungent aroma, and Bram advanced within the tree shadows. From inside the barn, the one-sided oratory continued. Was Willow inside? He couldn't be sure. He'd blow down the doors to rescue her if he could hear a solitary peep from his daughter.

With each step, Bram ducked and slithered behind a cluster of bushes, advancing nearer the barn. He focused on the speaker inside. An adult's voice—not some vagrant teenagers discussing their next bong hit. The voice stated bluntly:

"GPS it if you have to." A pause. "We're already here. Yeah. Twenty G's cash. No crypto and no checks." Silence. He cajoled, "The mutt's *your* problem." A perverse laugh. "A bullet costs a buck, right?"

The one-sided phone conversation ended. Bram dashed off a text to Lita: *Haunted barn. Need shotgun.* He muted his phone in case she called back. She'd respond on the double, whether she was two miles away or twenty. At least, he hoped so.

From where he stood in the shadows, Bram assessed his options. The words he'd heard were tipping points. "Ten o'clock. Cash. Dog. Bullet." Substantial money was involved, meaning multiple people, likely with dangerous weapons. The man inside would be armed, and Bram calculated his options. It was no time for heroics. Paternal rage, he understood, often required tempering. Barging in full commando with an iron bar might be akin to a death sentence. The guy inside could be military-trained, for all he knew. Or perhaps even worse, a desperate junkie with nothing left to lose.

No. Bram's rushing in like some O.K. Corral shootout was hardly a wise option.

He exhaled, calming himself. Stealth was a safer option. Especially with his young daughter caught potentially in the crossfire. He advised himself:

Assess your position, stick to facts, and work with what you know and don't. Slowly, a mental strategy began forming. As his training had taught, the chess pieces in his mind began aligning themselves in an orderly fashion.

Once his plan solidified, his fatherly rage would become an asset instead of a liability.

Bram assessed his weapons at hand. It helped having been inside the place earlier—he recalled the barn's inner layout. He had the crowbar, two fists, and a working brain. The metal bar didn't measure well against firepower. Facts were facts: no piece of pipe ever won a battle against a Colt .45.

Work with your strengths, maintain focus, and let the movie in your brain tell your body what to do.

At last, he had a strategy. Bram exhaled slowly from his concealed position in tree shadows and muttered to himself, "Where angels fear to tread."

He slipped forward with silent, cautious steps aided by the dampness. Ten feet from the barn's peeling front doors, he crouched and set his crowbar down in the weeds. He listened like a leopard. The man's voice rose and faded from inside the place, talking on his phone and perhaps pacing back and forth. No sound came from either the girl or the dog. They might be gagged, sedated, or possibly dead. *Don't even think it!*

Easing between the cracked doors, soundless, mindful of footsteps and sudden shifts in shadow, Bram remained crouched. He crept along the near wall to the farthest corner. Lowered to one knee, he listened to the man in the loft flapping his jaws like a tavern drunk. The man seemed enthralled by the echo of his voice.

Bram swept together a small pile of straw, hay, and dried burlap scraps, which he'd noticed were abundant across the dusty floor. He fished a Zippo from his inner jacket pocket. Cupping his hands, he held the tiny flame to the makeshift pile until the first wisps of smoke arose.

Quiet as a sigh, Bram slipped back out the barn door and into the somnolent night.

The guy was a windbag. Willow had stopped listening hours ago. But with his last few phone comments, she'd put the meaning of his words together. The tone painted a grim picture for both her and Clay. From how the guy talked, she was being sold to some evil men somewhere. And her pet dog, Clay, would be murdered. The man himself had joked, "A bullet costs a buck."

Her dad had instructed Willow on trusting her inner feelings and how it was her most significant survival skill.

"Your gut never lies," he had informed her repeatedly.

And now, Willow's gut told her she had to find a way to escape. To run for her life and pray they left her injured pet alone. She'd locate her dad, and they'd come back with his shotgun to save Clay.

Willow sat with her back against the rotted boards, her clothes and jacket filthy with dust and grime. No doubt a brown recluse lurked nearby, sizing her up like it would a big fat horsefly.

Clay lay close by, his breathing labored. A long cord was tied around his neck and secured to a leaning ceiling beam. He looked at her with moist eyes and whined. He lifted his snout and sniffed as if something wasn't right. Willow rose beside him and looked around the dark inside of the rotting barn. She coughed twice, and her eyes began to water. Stepping to the edge of the hayloft, she spotted the source—a small campfire of flames down below.

Her sudden hollers jarred the man on his phone to his senses. He moved across to where she stood, following her gaze down to the curling wisps of smoke. Sparks were igniting the scattered clumps of straw around the open lower floor. As they watched, the flames spread rapidly across the floor and began licking at the moldy wood of the barn's sidewalls.

"Son of a—" Horror filled the man's eyes, and the rising smoke made them water.

Clay's barking now caused Willow to rush back to his side. The slender man remained at the loft's edge, staring below at the scene as if paralyzed. "The ladder," he called out, turning his head back to Willow. He side-stepped his way along the high ledge. "Let's go! Now! Come on!"

"Not without Clay!" Willow's voice matched his demand. "I'm not leaving him here to die in a fire!"

Cory Mowry stood frozen with indecision. He didn't give a rat's rear end about the dog, but he needed the girl alive. She was his ticket out of the drug life that would soon destroy him if he remained. He glanced back again at Willow. Her thin arms were wrapped around the animal's neck, its eyes white with fear.

Flames skipped across the barn floor and climbed higher up the rotted wood, attacking the dry, wormy walls. Smoke rose like fog from a river. At last, coming to his senses, Mowry sprang into action. Kneeling beside the whimpering animal, he sliced the electrical cord around its neck with his jackknife. "There! He's free." He pointed wildly, rising and yanking Willow by the arm to the top of the hayloft ladder. The dog stood and barked behind them, refusing to budge, wary of the danger below.

"You have to carry him," Willow cried. "It's too high to jump."

Mowry studied the ladder and returned his eyes to the dog. The eighty-pound animal had an injured flank. It would snap at him if he tried lifting it. Yet, he also understood that the girl would be useless if he permitted her dog to perish. Become a shell, die inside herself.

"Down! Now!" he ordered. "I'll carry him right behind you."

"You better not be—"

"I promise."

With those words, he sprang into action, easing his way back to the canine. The animal bared his teeth and snarled at the man's approach.

Willow shouted, "Let him carry you, Clay! It's all right—be a good boy!"

Mowry hoisted the animal from underneath, using both his arms. It would be an effort to cart the dog down the ladder, but he was out of options.

"Get going!" he commanded Willow. He watched as she began descending the shaking ladder. She single-stepped down as fast as she dared. When the girl neared the bottom, Mowry started his climb down. He leveraged the weight of the whimpering animal against the inside ladder rungs to provide better balance. In less than a minute, his feet landed on the flame-spotted floor.

Coughing, her elbow to her face, Willow hopscotched toward the half-open barn door. The dog wormed itself free from his arms. It limped after her, oblivious to the spreading fire all around.

Mowry crocked his arm across his nose and wove his way after them. He watched them disappear through the smoky opening, escaping into the fresh air. Seconds later, holding his breath, Mowry shouldered the barn door wider and burst free of the death trap. He discerned the towering overgrowth of bushes and trees that formed a dark curtain at the edge of the clearing—all reflected orange by the flames they'd just escaped.

What Mowry failed to spot, however, was the shadow lurking to his left as he stumbled clear of the doors. Nor did he hear the whistle of iron arcing through the air, yet he did feel sudden pressure against the back of his skull that created an instant starburst of pain behind his eyes.

Even so, Mowry uttered no sound as his thoughts went dark, and he was unconscious before his face planted into the weed-covered turf.

Willow and Clay both collapsed to the ground fifteen yards from the barn doors. They choked and wheezed, laboring to take in the fresh air. Her vision was cloudy from the smoke, and the fiery heat washed over her in waves. Smoke seeped from every crack and orifice of the decrepit structure—wisps of rising vapor forming patterns in a choking cloud above them.

Spotting a shadow standing near the barn doors, Willow watched it toss a long object amid the unkempt weeds. The shadow proceeded to stride toward the kidnapper's unmoving body, and she witnessed the figure grab the prone man by his ankles. The unconscious body was dragged back to the fiery barn. The pair disappeared inside the crooked doors, which glowed orange from the intense inner heat.

Willow said in a faint voice, "It's the dragon mouth of Hell."

Behind her, she heard a pickup truck skid to a stop along the road's gravel shoulder. The engine was cut on the two-lane roadway opposite the clearing. High bushes blocked the truck's front half from view. A door slammed, and Lita emerged around the truck's back bumper. She held a shotgun, and her mouth was a grim slash. The leaping flames reflected demonically in her eyes as she surveyed the carnage.

At that exact moment, the shadow man reemerged from the barn. Willow turned and watched as he strode across the ground like walking through a graveyard, backlit by billowing smoke and flames. He picked up the weapon he had cast aside and marched toward her, advancing like a psycho in a horror film. Willow was too frightened to scream, having watched him drag the other man back into the inferno.

Tears seeped down her cheeks. She cowered against Clay's chest, holding him tightly. When the shadow finally stooped beside her, she released the dog and flung her arms around the man's hot, grimy neck.

"Daddy!" she wept, hugging him hard. "He almost . . . he was going to . . ."

Bram shushed her and stroked her hair with his large, earth-worn hands. He glanced across the weeds at Lita, who stood watching them through her tears before rushing forward to join them in happiness.

In a tender voice, Bram said to his daughter:

"Don't worry, sweet pea. He can't hurt us anymore."

Almost Died Event # 3 – SWING BLADE – age 13

The football skipped down the roof and short-hopped against the gutter. My eyes bulged when it halted on the neighbor's back lawn. It sat like a ticking hand-grenade. My blood froze. The significance of the trophy ball rang louder than a funeral knell. In a panic, I sprinted across our lawn and beelined toward the football. The old farmer burst from his shed carrying a garden hoe. He strode swiftly toward the ball. It would be decided by milliseconds, and I had a half-step advantage. The older man double-gripped the long handle. Dipping and swooping like a halfback, I scooped the ball as the sharp blade swept over my skull. I sped down the grassy path along the property's far side. Panting on the street, I carried the football beneath my arm as if returning a kickoff ninety-eight yards. I trotted up our driveway with my heart still tom-tomming. I peeked out our garage at the old farmer who paced inside his shed, cussing. His shadow reminded me of Ed Gein.

MIGHTY AL

Logline: When a spirited inventor wins a prestigious Intergalactic Award for creating his own planet in a research lab, he explains the uniqueness of his project to a captivated audience.

The massive inner ballroom is filled with guests in evening gowns and tuxedos. They sit clustered at linen-covered round tables of ten, chatting and laughing in low voices. They sip champagne and nod to one another, conversing, their half-smiles tucked beneath the occasional arched eyebrow.

The high electronic banner across the back of the large stage reads:

WELCOME TO THE 238th ANNUAL INTERGALACTIC CREATIVE ACHIEVEMENT AWARDS

The invitation-only crowd tonight consists of five-hundred guests. They are the top names in the arts, science, politics, and entertainment circles. The most creative and advanced minds across the galaxy have submitted their work. Trillions more viewers will watch the event via their internal Artificial Intelligence.

The tinkling of glasses dies down, and now, from the right emerges our MC. He is mid-aged with speckled gray hair. He wears a thousand-watt smile. His eyes dart and flicker playfully, a man who cracks jokes at the drop of a hat. We recognize him as the famous face of a hundred similar events.

Spotting his emergence, the crowd applauds, anticipating a laugh-filled and witty evening. The congenial host advances to center stage, bowing, preening, and mugging for them to continue approving. He mirrors their admiration. When the commotion quiets, he speaks into the microphone he holds.

"Thank you to everyone joining us here this evening. We bid you all welcome to the granddaddy of them all, the one and only ANNUAL CREATIVE ACHIEVEMENT AWARDS!"

Applause rings for a minute before dropping to respective silence.

"I'm Reeno McClintock, your humble ceremonial master tonight."

More smiles and clapping. Light laughter.

Three massive display screens behind him are set against the reception room's full-sized backdrop. We see different angles on Reeno as he prances across the boards.

Now, a trio of leggy supermodels, all dressed in clinging evening gowns, emerges from the wings. They are positioned together on the stage's left side. All are at least six-foot-seven in their spike heels. They tower over the MC, who feigns a cutesy soft shoe and bows to them gallantly.

He continues his banter. "So let's get to it. The moment we've all been waiting for."

The crowd murmurs drop. The models beam, their eyes fixed on the presenter.

"The revealing of our three finalists." He waits for the noise to diminish. "I will announce the two runners-up first. Then the judges' final verdict will reveal the new CREATIVE ACHIEVEMENT AWARDS WINNER for the year twenty-six-twenty-seven."

More cheers and excited applause follow, and virtual recording cameras pan to the massive visuals behind him, each capturing his generous toothy smile.

"But before we get to it all, allow me to thank everyone in attendance for the—he sotto-whispers to the audience around his palm—inconvenience we share by wearing our flesh suits tonight. It's very nostalgic to live here, knowing that thousands of star clusters in our galactic neighborhood have their vision orbs glued to this evening's spectacle."

Reeno faces the cameras and bows again before raising to full height. "On behalf of myself and the trillions of audience viewers, we thank everyone for joining us here this evening."

When the laughter and cheering subside, he barks out:

"But first, here's a word from our sponsors!"

~

Cut to a cluttered great room of a windowless, rustic cabin in the woods. There is a sink along one wall and a rumpled couch setting. A pair of back bedroom doors are closed. The kitchen table and surrounding chairs serve as a card table. The place is cluttered, and cleaning is not an obvious priority.

Four individuals are locked in a poker game at the table with cards fanned in their hands. A burly, silver-haired black man they call "Al" (sweatshirt and cargo shorts) sports a long ponytail. He's staring over a pair of reading glasses across the room at a muted, old-fashioned TV. He growls at the television, "C'mon, c'mon. Get on with it before hell freezes over."

Around him, the other three opponents study their hands. One is a smooth-haired twenty-something sporting a three-day stubble. He speaks without looking up. "Put a sock in it, Pops. We've got all eternity, don't we?"

"*You* put a sock in it, Sonny Boy." Al frowns, adding, "Besides, I've been grumpy all day."

"What? Your time of the month?" jokes Rust. He's the fourth player sitting with his back to the TV. His face is ruddy and sunburned, like a surfer on the water all day.

The two men laugh, and even Al cracks a stubborn smile. Their hi-jinks prompt a scowl from the player on Al's left. She's a willowy pale lady of curious gender, blessed with flowing blond hair and translucent, ghost-like skin. Her pale blue eyes are set above high cheekbones.

"Shush it. All of you," Marta warns. "I'm trying to think."

"Don't hurt yourself," says Sonny with a smirk.

"Yeah. Quit whining, Marta," Rust adds. "You haven't even ante'd this hand."

"I did so. If the pot's short, it's got to be—"

They all look toward Al, who groans and frowns. "Me again. Sorry." He slides three blue chips into the center heap. "Those TV bozos keep droning on and on."

"What about eternity, don't you get?" asks Sonny, amused. "The sound's off, anyway."

Rust winks at Marta. When she glares at him, he asks, "You betting or what?"

She slides two red chips into the pot with long fingers and issues them an airy look. Rust matches her wager, as do the others. Marta frowns at them one to the next.

"Going for the straight, are we?" Sonny asks this without looking at her.

She lays two cards face down. "Give me two."

Rust complies, and she scoops the new pair up with slender fingers.

"It's your tell," Sonny explains, casting a look her way. "Your cheeks flush when you've got a good hand."

The other players snicker. Marta pouts. The ponytailed Al slides in three matching chips, still barking at the TV, "Get on with it, for the love of... If I wanted to watch sidewalks crack—" To them all, he barks, "I hate *The Price is Right.*"

Sonny snickers. "You hate a lot of things."

"Ignorance, mostly." Al glances down at his cards. "Gimme two."

The ovation fills the cavernous ballroom. On stage, Reeno is applauding monkey-like at the audience. He announces into his mic, "Without further ado, let's introduce our two amazing runners-up."

The crowd is quieter than a fly's belch.

The face of an elderly Eurasian man appears on one of the giant upper screens. The MC says, "The second runner-up pioneered the concept of Reverse Quantum Travel, which, as you know, allows any of us to discard our flesh suits and traverse the galaxy at the speed of thought."

The audience *oohs* and *ahhs*. "As sentient, protoplasmic beings, we may now mind-port anywhere we choose. At the snap of our figurative fingers." He laughs, performing a finger snap. "So let's give it up for Professor TimLordo Cologne."

The gathered throng applauds with enthusiasm. Above them, the grinning man waves, winks, and disappears.

The cameras cut back to the host at the center front. He motions to quiet the crowd. "The top runner-up—" He turns from his mic, and on the high displays above, we see a weathered, white-haired lady in a wheelchair. She wears wire-rim spectacles. Her only otherwise distinctive feature is a dark Snidely Whiplash mustache.

Reeno projects his voice. "She discovered the reality of Negative Quark Entropy, proving her theorem that learning accelerates in living cells based upon their lack of the need for sleep. I give you a true game-changer in the field of advanced anti-somnolence, Miss MaPakitol Faye.

Vigorous clapping swells the banquet hall. The petite lady bows from her wheelchair. She vanishes from the giant overhead projections with a finger-twirl of her mustache.

The same rustic cabin in the night woods, with just a trio of players still at the poker table in the central room. Sonny glances up from his hand with a frown. He observes Al's empty chair, then turns to his left, watching Rust discard three cards.

"I'll take three," Rust says.

Sonny's look is tight. "We've got to wait until Al gets back."

"Are you sure he didn't drop out?" asks pale Marta.

"He just ran to the—"

"Pisser. He's in the pisser," Rust says crudely. "Isn't it the rule? You're out of the hand if you're in the pisser?"

Sonny shouts over his shoulder. "Hey, Al? You in or out?" The wide cabin shows papers strewn about, a sad pizza box where one wilted slice remains—discarded empty beer bottles. The old TV continues playing on its stand, the sound muted.

"Why's he make us call him 'Al'?" Marta asks.

"You saw his sweatshirt. It reads '*Mighty*,'" Sonny snickers, "with '*Al*' underneath it."

"Maybe for Al *Bodegas*?" Rust cracks, making them laugh. "The big meatball!"

A voice calls through the walls. "Hold your horses. Be there in a jiff."

The other three players grunt and study their hands. When Rust side-eyes Sonny, they smirk together. The muted voice calls again, "You punks better not be peeking at my cards."

"We're not peeking at nothing," Marta shouts back.

"Yeah. Quit being a stodgy old fart!"

Only to be replaced on the upper screens with the image of a sober, middle-aged black man. He wears dark-rim glasses, and his white hair is swept back and secured behind in a long, braided ponytail. He peers down at them with a stern, unblinking expression.

"And now, members of the Intergalactic Elite," MC Reeno says expansively. "And to everyone watching from across the cosmos." He pauses. "We've come to the highlight of the evening. The moment we've all been dying for."

The assembly holds its breath. He proclaims:

"I give you this year's winner of the Two-Hundred-Thirty-Eighth Annual: INTERGALACTIC CREATIVE ACHIEVEMENT AWARD."

A dramatic drum-roll thunders through the reception area, ending with the *crash* of cymbals.

Turning his head, the host grins up at the magnified image of the white-haired professor. In a bold voice, he announces:

"Dr. Alfonzo Osbunion DezRa."

Applause erupts from the audience. Reeno has to shout:

"Whom we've all come to know, simply, as Dr. Dez!"

And now our silver-haired winner emerges in person, entering from the wings. He's tuxedoed-up in light blue (sans bowtie) and strides to the center, offering half-waves, eyebrows arched as if surprised. A podium rises from the floor, and the two men shake hands beside it.

The ringing cheers continue with guests lifting to their feet: clapping, hair-flipping, toothy smiles, and fervent nods. At last, with Reeno's urging, the guests in their shimmering gowns and tuxedos sit back down. The buzzing and whispering dissolve.

Dr. Dez stands beside the celebrity presenter, who raises his microphone, saying, "We've learned of his story and followed his ambitious experiments in both the news forums and research journals." He turns to the doughy, ponytailed doctor, adding, "But here's a quick rehash."

The high monitors above them show multiple images of the doctor.

Reeno narrates: "Like a handful of others before him, Dr. Dez created his mini-universe in his laboratory. As a loose example, picture yourself looming over your private petting zoo." Mild laughter. "You—and you alone—control the temperature, the quality, and the lives of the species therein."

He adds, "The difference here is that Dr. Dez also *created* the animals. His pets, as it were. The old song goes, 'He used a hank of hair and a piece of bone...'" He welcomes the crowd's laughs before turning serious again. "Still, he took it a step further, didn't he? He designed his specimens with sentience, intellectual awareness, the morality of conscience, and ability to reason."

He glances at the doctor, who shrugs, and Reeno continues:

"So Dr. Dez, unlike other micro-universe designers, wasn't content to merely observe and measure the species in his zoo. No. His decision to instill himself into the equation sets him apart from researchers before him."

A few gasps emit during the pause.

"In other words," Reeno continues, "he revealed his *other-worldly* 'Creator' presence to his test group." More low-level noise amid the whispering. He further elaborates:

"The Doctor's hypothesis asked this: First, if you give any mammalian strain complete freedom of choice, will they accept you as the designer of their existence? And secondly, if you promise your creations eternal happiness, will they live by the principles you suggest for them?"

He pauses, allowing these questions to float through the massive entertainment hall.

"And third," he continues, reading his cue card. "Will your subjects accept they are not just flesh suits but also possess energy souls? Souls with consciousness and awareness? Souls that exist for eternity after the physical body has perished?"

He allows these precepts to penetrate the audience.

"And there we have it, my friends. Dr. Dez's experiment in a nutshell." Our dapper host adds, "Would these beings to whom he granted life accept him as their creator? Their guiding light, as it were? Or would they turn on him and allow chaos to rule their lives?"

Whispers sweep through the auditorium until, at last, he lifts his mic once more:

"Keeping in mind the premises I have explained, I now present to you this year's winner of the galaxy's CREATIVE ACHIEVEMENT AWARD . . . Dr. Alphozo Osbunion DezRa!"

Fervent cheers and shouts ring to the rafters as the onlookers shower praise. The overhead projections show the MC handing the doctor his prize—a glowing, translucent purple award with a beating heart hologram lodged inside. The doctor accepts the pulsating item, and at the podium, he turns to face the beaming audience. The standing ovation continues. He raises the trophy high, offering them a sheepish half-smile, his ponytail swaying behind him.

Reeno backs toward the stage wing, receding away while he continues clapping. Alone at the podium, Dr. Dez leans toward the microphone as the clamor quiets.

"Don't be alarmed, my friends." He grins warmly. "I'll keep my comments brief."

Another splash of sauterne laughter, their smiles climbing the high auditorium walls.

The enamored guests sit back down, ready to be entertained.

Silence now. A cough or two.

"There are a few questions," Dr. Dez begins, "everyone asks about my project." He looks side to side, roping them all in. His voice is stark and reverberates throughout the room. "First, my research team consists of four of us, including myself. Your AI can download the bios of my colleagues—if you're interested." He pauses to allow them to do so. "The second question is often this: what was our project about? Truly about? What was the point of the experiment? Its theme?"

After a dramatic silence, he shrugs and adds, "Allow me to explain the details."

He exhales for another beat and continues:

"We created a virtual, quantum-holographic universe. Essentially, it is an expansive, oxygen-capable terrarium to simplify it. Then, we added an enclosed, modular, interplanetary system. And at its nexus, we created a planet, which I chose to call Earth." He waits, allowing the audience's AI to access all this from the formularies.

"So, how long did it take to create this mini-universe?" He pauses. "In 'Earth time,' we set the planet to appear at over four-billion years old. In our current time-construct, however—yours and mine—we began this project about ten months ago. From conception to reality. We published the results eight weeks ago—seven days before the contest submission deadline."

He laughs along with the audience, nodding and smiling across the ballroom. Someone whistles and scores a few chuckles.

"Where, then, was this solar system created?" Dr. Dez pauses a beat. "We fashioned our laboratory's enclosed holographic structure in the techno-quadrant of the planet Fostuma—where we currently sit."

He glances around. "From your perspective, my lab is roughly the size of this stage. Earth's solar system, therefore, was created inside a twenty-by-thirty-yard oxygenated chamber, with the planet's dimensions about the size (to us) of a marble." Dr. Dez exhales. "We created a quantized, Bosonic-designed hologram of the planet, consistent with their (meaning human subjects) standing on an actual soil surface: mountains, sky, seas, the whole works. Complete with water, gravity, and atmosphere. A revolving moon, sun, and the surrounding physicality of space and energy."

He allows the imagery to sink in.

Dr. Dez then adds, "I employed old-fashioned, dark mater-entanglement virtual reality-ware to create a time-space continuum for our inhabitants. Thus, to better enhance the illusory effect."

Heads bob in the educated audience.

"So why do all this in the first place?" Dr. Dez's eyes narrow behind his spectacles. He continues:

"As MC Reeno mentioned in the intro, my team and I had a singular premise. We wanted to design a subspecies (called human beings, or humankind, if you will) who were creative, clever, multi-linguistic, and of sentient nature." He waits for his words to settle. "I wondered if we allowed this experiment of group free will—to either believe in a higher power (a divine creator) or reject the idea—well, which path would they choose to follow?"

Silence as the guests search their AI.

The doctor continues. "And lastly, how would we quantify our results?"

He allows the questions to hang in the air.

"And here's where the plot thickens." He pulls in a few laughs. "I decided the best way to test my hypothesis was to interject myself—revealed to them as their 'Divine Creator Being'—into the scenario. This idea allowed me to function as both an arbitrator of justice as week as an active participant."

After a somber moment, he adds, "I rejected the idea of being some mysterious God-Energy lurking hidden behind an invisible curtain. I instead wanted to reveal my true nature to the beings I created, informing them I was indeed the creative force behind their existence—the *designer* of their Universe. By doing so, I was allowing them a seat at the proverbial table, as it were."

An audible buzz sweeps over the room. When it dies down, the doctor continues:

"You might now ask, 'Wouldn't they recognize at some point that they were living in a virtually generated simulation?'" The doctor shakes his head. "Since their reality was physical, and they possessed conscious freedom of thought—to each enjoy personal hopes and dreams—and I was an actual presence, and not some mythical cloud-dweller with six arms, so that reality to them was no simulation. How could it be? The world they occupied was solid. Taste, hear, touch, smell, see." He adds, "From their perspective, their existence was as real as I'm standing before you right now."

Dr. Dez reaches below and sips from his water bottle to prove his point.

Nodding heads. Whispers along with understanding smiles. He continues: "How, then, did we assess my hypothesis?"

Dr. Dez pauses. "Remember—we're talking about free will here. Their freedom to choose their own beliefs." He continues, "Thus, I revealed I was an actual metaphysical entity. And secondarily, I then provided our subjects with a moral code to live by.

His eyes search the crowd. "We called it my Ten Commandments," he adds, "and I hand-delivered it to one of their leaders. I inscribed it in stone so there could be no doubt."

Dr. Dez half-turns and directs their attention to the trio of elevated displays behind him. A gigantic hand extends down from the clouds with a vague image of Dr. Dez behind it. He extends down a pair of giant stone tablets to a bearded older adult garbed in robes.

Murmurs lift from the audience.

"If they lived by this modest code," the doctor adds, "after their flesh bodies degraded, I promised their souls would be rewarded with an eternal spiritual afterlife. A peaceful existence of nirvanic bliss with all the friends they once had during their lives."

Silence grips the room.

"But if they chose instead to reject me," he adds, his voice rising, "their energy souls would be snuffed out like fairy dust. *Poof*!" He snaps his fingers like a magician. "Very elementary parameters, I'm sure you would agree." He shrugs nonchalantly. "This seemed like a fair and humane choice—the lady or the tiger? As some might say."

He presses a button on the background screen remote. This time, a colorful video appears on the overheads. It shows the Earth being flooded by violent, torrential storms. A lonely, solitary, but sizeable wooden ship is seen bobbing atop the undulating waters.

"And yet, only one man seemed to play by the rules. His name was Noah."

The audience members study their internal AI for reference.

"As you might speculate," continues the silver-haired doctor, "the subjects seemed not to comprehend the very principles of the game."

He extinguishes the video stream and turns back to face the crowd.

"Noah informed his offspring why their planet Earth had been flooded," he explains. "Humans had inherited the sins of their fathers. Lies, wickedness, corruption, and the worship of false idols. Amid other deviances." His smile is crooked. "I decided their world needed a *divine* reset."

The audience seems intrigued by the story. "To further this endeavor, I created prophets for our humans—individuals who foretold how future events would unfold if they did or didn't follow the game plan. These prophets spread my *word*. And they also offered them a road map toward spiritual enlightenment."

Coughs are heard, and chairs shuffle. Dr. Dez presses forward.

"And yet, despite all these efforts, I could see the lessons still weren't getting through to these humans. Allowing this arrogant species the will to choose whatever nonsense they concocted was not working the way I'd hoped—and sin seemed to be their default mode." He lowers his tone. "Many of them lied, cheated, and practiced perversions almost daily. The punishment of the flood seemed all but forgotten."

The doctor's lips tighten.

"Thus," he confesses, "I decided that more dramatic measures were required."

Someone in the audience stifles a yawn, and a few guests giggle.

Dr. Dez aims the remote, illuminating the background image screens with winter night skies. A single shooting star flickers across the heavens.

"So, I gave them the gift of my son—born of the human race." His smile is fatherly. "We named him *Yeshua*." He pauses while their AI researches this. "He would preach among them, comfort them, provide them with a moral compass to follow. My son would perform miracles in my honor to show them the desired path toward honesty and goodness."

Dr. Dez pauses, adding, "As a bonus, the birth of Yeshua would wash away all the sins of their pasts. So they all had a clean slate if they chose."

Across the audience, eyebrows arch at the concept.

Dr. Dez clicks the remote, and the screen images shift. The guests view the painful depiction of a slender man being marched through a town and tortured. His limbs are nailed to a wooden cross before it's raised and stabbed upright into a nearby hill. An audible gasp lifts from the seated crowd.

A lady at a third table row cries, "You mean they murdered him? Yeshua? Those low-life imbeciles slaughtered your son?"

Angry murmurs rise, abhorrence mixed with confusion.

Another man's voice shouts, "What kind of heathen savages are these humans?"

"Allow me to answer that." The doctor's eyes sweep the crowd. "Their problem, it seemed, wasn't so much with free will. It was their lack of a moral compass."

Heads nod across the spacious room.

"My team and I gathered for a brainstorming session. We decided a written manual was what our subjects needed—something concrete. A book to read and refer to, instead of relying on verbal stories and old tales to spread my ideas."

He adds, "Aided by AI, we composed the entire tome in a day."

Heads turn to one another, smiling. They have never existed for a minute without AI to guide them.

"I desired this book to be mysterious, symbolic, and spoken in multiple voices to avoid sounding preachy. Poetic, yet conveyed in story form. It had a set-up, a theme-related midpoint, and a startling, good-versus-evil conclusion."

Heads nod at the familiar formula. They've seen it a billion times before.

"We named it the *Holy Bible*. Why not? If I'd had an agent or publisher, you bet they'd have come up with something catchier." The spectators laugh amusedly. Dr. Dez adds,

"It was intended as a user's manual for living decent lives. Not harming one another. A roadmap filled with lessons and parables."

On the elevated screens, a leather-bound book image is shown. It appears unwieldy to a crowd unfamiliar with physical books, beings used to internal AI downloads where text is imprinted instantaneously into their cortices.

"Earth time passed," the doctor says with a sigh. He fobs his slide advance button, and the large screen displays behind him show a giant Nephilim fallen angel raping a pair of Earth women.

A roar of laughter emits from the crowd, and it causes Dr. Dez to turn and look upward at the images. With a frowning blush, he quickly advances the slide.

"Whoops," he says sheepishly, turning back to them. "That one wasn't supposed to be in there."

The titters and laughter slowly diminish. Several attendees scurry to probe their AI for the word "Nephilim."

Beneath his breath, Dr. Dez curses, "Dammit, Rust! Always the prankster." He feels his forehead warm but regains his composure and presses on gamely with his speech.

"Religious scholars and monks," he conveys, "hand-copied our holy book. To hasten things, I taught them printing and mass distribution. The Bible proved an enormous success. It became the first bestseller in planet Earth's history."

Images appear on the upper projections. They show millions of people reading the Good Book on their own, at ceremonies and gatherings, or in small family sessions during holidays.

A voice in the crowd calls out: "How about more Nephilim?" A man in the third row takes a cutesy bow as hoots and laughter again fill the ballroom.

Dr. Dez curses beneath his breath: *Damn you, Rust. I'll get you back for that.*

"By this time," he continues unabashedly, "my son's followers had created a growing movement. His sacrifice had not been in vain after all. He had amassed quite a large congregation of true believers."

Dr. Dez's shoulders droop as if the death of his son *Yeshua* continues to haunt him. He flashes a series of images above on the high displays and glances back to ensure another of Rust's pranks doesn't appear. He continues:

"Our Bible showed the Earth inhabitants a path to living simple and righteous lives. Obeying moral rules and practicing kindness became the essence of spirituality. Vast numbers of this test group were now bathed in the glow of their creator. Massive cathedrals and gothic churches were constructed around the globe, imbued with blazing rainbow-colored windows. All designed to honor my son and me."

The doctor gazes at the audience, a hint of melancholy showing behind his dark-frame glasses. "In other words, my experiment was back on track."

He again senses a restlessness in the audience, as if they have somewhere more pressing to be. Perhaps more vigorous action in this speech is required. Well, he can provide action with the best of them. He silently cautions them, *Be patient, my friends. It's a virtue.*

Casting his eyes out, Dr. Dez studies the crowd. These are the hoity-toity of the cosmos, the interstellar rich and famous. They are the great movie and stage performers of their galaxy. Many are politicians and wealthy business magnates; others are military leaders, scientists, smug newscasters, bureaucrats, and shadowy consultants. However they define themselves, they are all members of the same universal cabal.

They are the ruling class. You know them as the "One-percenters."

These are the status-seekers, those who attend stiff-necked events like this one. It is a crowd (in the doctor's humble opinion) who view celebrity and self-importance as the ultimate end-all. They see themselves as genetically superior, their IQs cleverer, each far more gifted than the unpolished masses. These are the movers and shakers of this particular cosmos—society's chosen bluebloods who have risen to the top of the heap.

His inner voice reminds him, "And oh, how their self-important drivel becomes annoying after a while."

Dr. Dez clears his throat, prepared to resume his acceptance speech, yet his same inner voice further asks, "As slaves to their AI, does even one of them comprehend what 'free will' honestly means?"

Alas, he reels himself back to the point. "So, now for the juicy parts," he teases, letting the polite chuckles dissipate.

"Things went well for almost two centuries through human wars, plagues, and famines. Until it seemed the success of my book had run its course." He sighs. "Our subjects eventually returned to their non-compliant ways, trading proof of my existence for mystical science and crackpot ideas. In every way they could manage, time and again, their innate desire was to participate in deviant activities."

He frowns at the audience.

"My efforts had fallen short once more. Did I wonder if perhaps this species hadn't been challenged enough? Not put through the wringer? And did the soup require, perhaps, more spice?" His voice echoes. "And thus, I stirred the pot further by allowing evil to rear its ugly head again."

"And I assure you," he adds, "this was not an easy decision."

The doctor gives them an honest look.

"Although he was a solid player during this first half of our experiment, I allowed Satan—a nemesis I had created—free rein over the entire planet. He could quantum-accelerate his role as the tempter. I allowed him his private legion of demons for assistance, and they had my permission to create as much havoc as they desired."

The crowd shifts restlessly, whispering among themselves.

"And yes, my friends. I *allowed* this to happen. If it's the devil they wanted, it's the devil they'd get."

On the overhead screens, we see a reinvigorated Lucifer perched high on a mountaintop. He watches fires, explosions, rolling tanks crushing innocents, and rifles firing. He witnesses the slaughter of fleeing villagers as they attempt to escape from an overwhelming force of jack-booted soldiers.

"War, death, fighting... backstabbing, jealousy, and murder." The doctor pauses. "These became the traits of humankind across the world. "And in individual homes, it was no better. Envy and bitterness. Resentment and arguments. Substance abuse, lying, physical harm."

He sighs. "They all ran rampant as Satan and his invisible army of demons went about corrupting people's hearts."

The crowd before him is silent.

"After letting things play out for a while, I decided this had to cease. Perhaps what my subjects required," I reasoned, "was an increase in technology—nuclear energy, perhaps aided by a computer revolution. Our test group would emerge from this dark period of war and oppression—wouldn't they?—if I allowed them greater intellectual freedom. Enlightened their existence with technological breakthroughs."

A dozen knowing heads nod. It makes absolute sense.

"The gift of technology appeared short-lived, however. Somewhat predictably, this test species, in short order, returned to their default mode of sin and perversion. Money and sex were at the root of their deviance." Dr. Dez sighs resignedly.

"These techno advances had been designed for enlightenment," he emphasizes. "But instead, they were used to create thermonuclear bombs and computerized porn."

A groan emits from the crowd amid a few snickers.

"Another decade passed in Earth time," the doctor continues, "mere days for us. My colleagues and I accepted our mistakes." His smile is tepid. " They now possessed nuclear technology and were advancing rapidly. Thus, the logical next step was to give them their own AI. A pre-school version."

Grins and applause ring through the elegant hall. To the crowd's way of thinking, any lifeform without artificial intelligence is akin to farmers trudging over fields behind draft horses or homemakers using butter churns.

"I admit my motives were selfish." Dr. Dez shrugs. "On an altruistic level, one might argue that I did this for the greater good—to help their race advance into the twenty-third century. "Yet on the other hand . . ."

He spreads his palms. "We all, here, understand the capabilities of reverse-matter virtual-construct AI. And having produced the greatest book in human history—my own story, no less—I understood how computerized marketing could reach millions of potential new converts."

The doctor gives them time to absorb the concept.

"Therefore," he says, "we relaunched our *Holy Bible*. This time online, to guide this civilization toward kindness and humility and further away from Satan's influence toward deviance.

Scattered clapping.

"We created landing platforms and hi-def sites." He aims his power pointer up at the displays behind him. Multiple scrolls of text flash past, eons of biblical information. "We received massive uploads by readers and listeners and an influx of hungry new converts. We stopped counting at over sixty-million hits on our sites."

The ballroom viewers witness pages scrolling faster and texts flying by at a dizzying pace.

"Our team labored day and night measuring interest and crunching numbers. After a while, however, we hit the brick wall. Enthusiasm dwindled again and spiraled downward. Until finally, well, reality slapped us in the face."

Dr. Dez waits as they scan their AI for answers.

"We had failed as before." His shoulders slump, and frustration colors his words. "Forced to admit defeat." He pauses. "The sad reality was—Satan had beaten us at the technology game. The human lust for evil seemed to triumph over the Golden Rule."

His lips are pressed while staring out at the quiet crowd.

"Computers. Mobile phones. Artificial Intelligence. They had invaded every household. Entire nations became enthralled."

He sweeps one arm out. "Information gluttony. Trapped by their devices, individuals ceased talking face-to-face. Emotions were inflamed by disinformation. Churches and schools became obsolete as corrupt political elites shunned worship and education. Millions of jobs and careers ended. Educators became politicized and diminished. Foolish know-it-alls were allowed predominant voices, spreading both idiocy and untruths."

His exasperation deepens as he presses on. "Hospitals closed as plagues and disease flourished—many outbreaks made-up or manufactured in laboratories by greedy pharmaceutical companies. Physical contact and exercise became old-fashioned concepts. All made worse by the increase in self-driving vehicles and a variety of sleek robotic companions."

The doctor turns to the screens, and we witness Satan (disguised, of course) addressing the United Nations General Assembly. He is amused, it seems, at the vacuous version of humanity he has molded to his liking.

"Lies and deceit," the doctor continues, "masked by the half-truths of newsfeeds. Falsehoods were spread about politics, finance, world events, and disease. Lies poisoned brother against sister, men against neighbors, states against nations."

The crowd sits uncomfortably silent.

"Our subjects were trapped by ignorance. They surrendered their free will, becoming infected by groupthink. They marched to the edicts of government bureaucrats, who had become power-hungry pawns. Satan's cabal of global billionaires remained the puppet masters, manipulating the strings behind the scenes.

Silence held the great hall in its grip.

At the stage's edge, the trio of supermodels exchanges tight looks. Yet their gleaming grins never drop in wattage. Dr. Dez scans the audience. His diatribe over, he offers a wan smile. "And now, how about if we lighten the mood?"

The relieved audience sighs.

"Technology became their new god," the doctor states, standing taller. "People had discarded their maker—the almighty entity who had promised their souls' eternal peace and happiness. Their reasons seemed fanciful. Just as their ancestors had worshipped golden calves and statues of Baphomet long ago, the species again turned its back on salvation. They had chosen greed, filth, and corruption over humility, kindness, and family values. All played out nightly on their televised news."

His voice becomes sterner. "When their leaders were questioned about the society's apparent corruption and downfall, they shouted back: 'We are enlightened beings of the Universe! God is just a Santa Claus fairytale. Only *provable* science is what we believe!'"

The doctor cynically adds, "Despite the science I'd given them, their silly beliefs contained gaping holes in evidence and logic."

Pin-drop quiet across the ballroom.

"What drivel," he says with disgust. "Instead of believing in the miracle of Christmas, they elected to worship one shiny ornament on the tree. One that reflected their distorted faces."

He shakes his head in dismay and continues:

"Millions of human beings had rejected me—the designer of their Universe. They rejected my son, sent to offer them hope, and also discarded my promise of reuniting their souls with their loved ones in the afterlife."

He adds resignedly, "My experiment, it seemed, had proved a failure."

Shuffling chairs and low coughs echo across the hall.

"And now, my friends, for the climactic finish I promised you." He sighs. "With few choices remaining, I unleashed Armageddon. It was the ultimate battle between humanity's two staunchest adversaries—Satan's demonic forces pitted against my Legion of Angels, led by my warrior son Yeshua. Across the Earth and sky, we would clash."

The elevated stage screens show images of a flat expanse of land between tall mountain ranges. Two great armies face one another. With the ultimate battle set, trumpets sound to commence the charge.

"Across earth and sky, they battled, with my troops forcing the enemy to *Feel my wrath!*"

The audience watches the clash unfold in quantum color, cringing at the violent carnage of massive fires, exploding warheads, and giant roaring beasts consumed by bloodlust. Bullets and bayonets flash with fury as opposing warriors rush into the fray, chorused by the *cracking* of a hundred-thousand machine guns. Torn limbs and scorched flesh meld melodiously together, blending the horrific screams of the innocent with the agonized shrieks of the dying.

"Of course," the doctor adds soberly, "this bloody conflict had been predicted centuries earlier (Earth time). Foretold in prescient detail in our Bible's *Book of Revelation*. Which their leaders had laughed away as 'myth.'"

Guests squirm in their chairs. A handful flees from the hall, unable to stomach such graphic violence. Nevertheless, this is one awards presentation their AI won't soon forget.

"As a result," Dr. Dez summarizes, "Satan and his minions—man and beasts alike—were defeated and cast down into the firepits of hell."

More nauseating images play on the high visual screens until, at last, he clicks the remote, and the projections behind him vanish.

"And thus, my friends, this project was complete." He surveys the crowd. "So I ask you now, what, if anything, did our experiment reveal?"

Blank expressions stare back. Until a solitary voice calls out: "Don't mess with Mother Nature!"

Uneasy laughter fills the ballroom.

"Close." The doctor ropes them with his gaze. "How about 'Don't mess with Mother Nature's *Father?*' The one who created her in the first place."

Uncertain eyes gaze back at him.

"Given the answers to life's mysteries ahead of time, what did these Earthlings choose?" Dr. Dez answers it for them. "They elected to chase their tails into oblivion." His voice echoes. "I might add, in a pitiable downward spiral."

He turns his head and the gray ponytail sways.

"I had given them an easy choice: 'Obey a few quaint rules, and your souls will live on in eternal bliss.' Yet, stubbornly, they chose the door where the hungry tiger awaited inside."

Silence captures the ballroom.

"I had manufactured their Universe using entanglement holograms and virtual-dimension reality. Even so, they doubted my presence because the rudimentary mathematics I'd allowed them could not 'prove' my existence."

His eyes pierce the crowd.

"I'd created my humans in my image, placing them in a glorious garden called Eden. Yet their scientists, using corrupted data, preferred telling their fellow brethren they were little other than the descendants of 'tree-apes.'"

The high-class audience chuckles.

"Nevertheless, even tree apes had to be created by *someone*." He scans the crowd. "And the final insult was that the more educated and advanced our humans became, the higher their stupidity levels rose." He allows this to sink in. "I had proven my reality to them by giving them their existence, despite many of them being too naive to accept this truth."

Audience members exchange looks.

"Perhaps most frustrating of all," the doctor continues, "was their pursuit of *How* and *When* they were created." His shoulders stiffen. "Their most important question should have been, by *Whom*? Who had created their reality? Who could take it away in an instant?"

He snaps his fingers to emphasize the point.

"Let me wrap things up now with a simple postulation."

Dr. Dez's tone becomes more playful. "Have you ever played an ancient card game called stud poker?"

He waits as their AI searches. A few hands are raised.

"My example is this." His eyes narrow. "After an opening deal, one player states they hold three aces. The other players must decide if it's a bluff or not." He stares out at nodding heads. "My experiment concluded this way. Many subjects chose to believe in me, and their souls advanced to the next level. Others, however, convinced themselves it was all a bluff—and if you listen closely, you can hear the screams of their flesh frying in the oil pans of eternal damnation right now."

An uneasy shuffling of chairs.

"Why would so many of these beings opt not to have their souls live forever? Surrounded by their families and loved ones? When all they had to do was follow a few polite rules?"

Dr. Dez spreads his hands. "Stubbornness? Ignorance? Lack of imagination?" He pauses. "Or perhaps they were deliberately misled by those who enjoyed spreading falsehoods?"

He shrugs resignedly. "Either way, I suppose the simple answer is, 'God only knows.'"

Unease was palatable across the ballroom. Dr. Dez reaches for his glimmering award, which has been tucked until now on a low podium shelf. He pulls it free for them all to see.

"My dear friends, I will leave you to ponder these strange mysteries." In conclusion, he adds, "Many thanks, and I bid you each a wonderful evening."

Hearty applause follows, with smiling patrons rising like clapping seals to show appreciation for this year's winner. The doctor hoists his translucent trophy in one hand, nodding his thank-yous. He strides past the trio of applauding supermodels, exiting stage right to the serenade of murmured voices and shuffling chairs.

Offstage, with the lighting people and assistant organizers stepping aside, Dr. Dez gives them a wave of thanks. He descends a small set of steps. Echoing behind him, he hears Reeno the MC's voice reverberating through the ballroom:

"And that, ladies, gents, and others, concludes another amazing awards event for . . ."

Striding away like a pro wrestler from the ring, Dr. Dez snaps the fingers of his free hand. The entire motif—backstage, auditorium, flesh-suited laborers, audience, building, everything (except for his award)—vanishes instantly.

Just as suddenly, Al emerges from the edge of a night forest, again wearing his sweatshirt, cargo shorts, and high tops. Aided by pale moonlight, he strides toward the door of a rustic cabin, where he enters without knocking.

The same three players sit at the poker table in the expansive central room. The flushing toilet noise causes Sonny to glance up from his hand. He frowns at the older man's approach.

"Took you long enough," Sonny complains.

"Yeah, prostate issues?" jokes Rust, causing them to giggle.

Marta rolls her eyes.

"Drain the weasel," says Al, his silver ponytail swaying as he approaches them. His comment prompts a laugh from Rust, who rocks back in his chair with his flushed face grinning.

Marta asks, "Are you in or not, Al? We haven't got all night."

The burly man resumes his spot at the table. He picks up his cards and studies them, his reading glasses low on his nose. "What's the bet again?" he asks without looking up.

"Three red," says Rust.

"It's three blue," Marta corrects. "I put in three blue."

Sonny says, "You bet three red—I saw you."

"You're both crazy."

The trio begins bickering, claiming this and that, barking at one another.

A second later, Al flips his cards face-up on the table. They stare at his trip aces, then up to his smirking face. He snaps his fingers, and they vanish entirely together. The deck and chip piles have also disappeared. Three empty table chairs highlight the cluttered room with the old TV still spinning reruns of "The Price is Right."

Al's ponytail sways as he rises from his chair. He turns to the nearby bedroom door and opens it. He mumbles as he steps inside. "Like I said, I woke up grumpy this morning."

He closes the door, disappearing into the bedroom. Despite his exit, the great room remains lit up by the glow of the muted, continuously running TV.

Almost Died Event # 4 – LOCKER DEATH TRAP – age 14

I was fifteen and in ninth grade. A scrawny one hundred twenty pounds. It was late February and cold outside, so I wore a heavy blue parka. We finished basketball practice in the old junior high. Our locker room had tall lockers, and we were the last two players lingering. My friend Fred dared me to try fitting inside a locker with my heavy coat on. Accepting the challenge, I slipped inside the metal unit, and he closed it. I was unable to unlatch it from within. He laughed at the prank. After a minute, I began shouting and begged him to open it. I was perspiring heavily from the exertion of practice, and with the heavy coat, I was starting to panic. I called his name through the vent. "Please let me out, Freddy! Please! I'm not kidding!" I was near passing-out. My desperate voice must have convinced him. He was already dressed and left after opening the locker. I tumbled out and fell to the concrete floor. I'd have suffocated within five more minutes if he'd left me inside with no one else around.

Almost Died Event # 5 – BRAIN BLEED – age 18

A sunny May afternoon. As a slender high school senior, I was the city's reigning pole vault champ. My friend Shep was also an excellent vaulter. Our coach excused us from school mid-afternoon for a few practice vaults. Our classmates peered from the second-floor windows and watched. Showing off. I set the bar at 12'6" and soared over it. I landed on the matt's back edge, whipping my head against the hard ground. We returned inside for our final school period. I felt strange in class and was confused and dizzy at my locker. The bell sounded. I went down to our locker room. Someone alerted Coach that I didn't seem right. Shep told them I had hit my head. Coach called my mom, and they drove me to the ER. The doctors diagnosed a concussion; the X-rays showed a "brain bleed." I had to remain bedridden for three days. I was to report if my vision went dark and I couldn't walk or talk. They said I'd be fine in a few days. To me, "brain bleed" sounded far worse than a concussion. Even a healthy kid like me could die by morning if it reoccurred at night.

On the runway three days later, I soared through the air again. My dad had sagely told me, "You've got to get back up on the horse that threw you."

SHE'S SOMETHING ELSE

Logline: When Interpol agent Mina Wilton trails a suspected Liberian sex-trafficker to the U.S., she soon discovers she's out of her league when going toe-to-toe against a powerful voodoo priest.

It was a long shot, one in a hundred. But people had hit paydirt against far greater odds. So Mina shrugged and told herself it was at least worth a try.

She sat on a country road in her white Saab rental and studied the ritzy home through her field glasses. It was a wonderous estate whose curving drive-up led to the circular front. The three-story mansion was red brick with tall cathedral windows. However, unlike most English countryside estates where Mina had grown up, there was no gated entry. This was the American Midwest, the landscape vast, and not a wealthy country squire in sight.

From a distance, the Crenshaw Estate appeared more castle than home. It sat nestled amid meadows and farmlands overlooking a winding river. The Saturday afternoon party celebrated Marla Crenshaw's thirty-fifth birthday. Several close friends were gathered in the backyard, chatting on the low-walled patio outside the house's back.

Interpol Agent Mina Wilton was two thousand miles from her office in Lyon, France. She was playing a hunch. She'd been tailing Liberian Colonel Tazeki Mabutu for nearly six months. He ran a sex trafficking ring that sold African children to perverts in the United States, Canada, the Virgin Islands, and every continent that paid cash for his goods as a modern-day slave trader. Mina never suspected that she'd wind up on a Saturday afternoon in June in the Upper Midwest U.S., a mere two miles outside Green Bay, Wisconsin, of all places.

Mina set aside the field glasses. She shifted the Saab into gear, proceeded up the winding front driveway, and parked on the lawn's edge beneath the shade of sturdy Dutch elm. Exiting, a butler-like college student answered the bell—likely working for cash and tips. Once inside, Mina grabbed a glass of champagne from a server's tray and was shown down the long hallway. Huge, open-door rooms braced each side until she was escorted onto the crowded outside patio.

"You must be the professor?" Marla Crenshaw cooed, shaking hands with the blond-haired Mina.

"Gretchen Loman," Mina lied, matching her smile. "I'm Julia's—"

"Aunt. From London, right?" The ladies laughed together. Marla said, "So happy you could make it."

Mina's eyes searched the guests for her make-believe aunt. "Julia's run off with Reese," Marla added. "Something with their youngest." Her eyes narrowed. "Nothing serious. Said she'd be back in twenty minutes."

Mina nodded, watching as Marla turned and called, "Toby! Please check on what the kids are up to."

Thirty feet away, a lean man in eyeglasses waved back. He stepped onto the open lawn, where six children had gathered around a koi pond.

"My husband, Tobias," Marla announced. "He promised to watch them while I play hostess."

Marla excused herself and stepped away in the opposite direction. Mina wandered about making small talk, waiting (she claimed) for her cousin Julia to return. She wound up a short distance from a large boathouse, content to linger at the party's periphery. She observed the man of the house, Tobias, rejoining his circle of casually garbed friends.

An unseen male voice called loudly: "I hear a pervert is lurking around here, preying on innocent women?"

The sudden voice startled Tobias. Looking around the group, his eyes bulged as the speaker approached.

"Tazeki?" Tobias said unsteadily. "What are . . . is it honestly you?"

Colonel Tazeki Mabutu, Mina noted, was garbed in charcoal summer-weight slacks and a gray mock turtleneck. Fifth Avenue cocktail chic. He closed in, and the two men warmly shook hands.

"You were expecting Nelson Mandela?" Mabutu joked.

The other men around Tobias laughed jocularly. Tobias stammered, "It's just that—"

The dark-skinned visitor hugged Tobias warmly. Doing so, he whispered, "Stop staring. I'm not quite a ghost yet, am I?"

Mina noticed a perspiration sheen across Tobias's brow. "What are you doing here?" he asked in a muffled voice, glancing suspiciously around them.

Mabutu's voice remained calm. "A social call to my old college roommate. It's not taboo, I hope?"

Tobias stepped back, smiling at his nearby friends. A few heads had turned, and perhaps they wondered: *Who is this slick foreign visitor? A celebrity? A new Packers' assistant coach?*

Mabutu ignored their curious faces. He said low to Tobias, "Perhaps they think I'm your gardener?"

Tobias forced another laugh as if the visitor's joke was a cracker. He remained jittery, nervous.

Twenty feet away, Mina thanked the server for a champagne refill as a pair of chatty females approached her. While politely smiling and shaking hands, she kept her ears tuned to Tobias and Colonel Mabutu. Of course, Mina had memorized the entire Interpol file on the Liberian military leader. The man was a high-ranking government official who controlled an elite unit of security forces. More importantly, he operated the most lucrative human trafficking ring on the African continent.

Tobias Crenshaw, however, was a mystery to her Interpol dossier. Mina had read that he was one of Mabutu's friends from back in their college days. Yet now, there seemed a strain between the two men. Perhaps because the Colonel had dropped in unexpectedly. *Very curious*, Mina noted, acting as though she and the chatting pair of ladies were old friends who hadn't seen one another in ages.

Mabutu, of course, was traveling under the radar this far from his home base. Mina was pleased that her organization had nailed the intelligence, and she hadn't wasted her trip chasing bott flies. As she chatted amicably with the ladies, she spotted Marla Crenshaw gliding gracefully up to join her husband and his former college chum. Her blond bangs rendered her a youthful appearance, her golden earrings dangling. Marla possessed an undercurrent of sensuality as she extended her hand to greet the new visitor. Mabutu smiled graciously at her and added the faint bow of a diplomat.

Everyone grinned except Tobias, whose left eyelid was now twitching. He excused himself from the group, admitting that he required eyedrops, and hastened toward the house's back entrance. Trailing after him the way ladies often visit restrooms in pairs, Mabutu followed.

The scene intrigued Mina. She used their departure as an excuse to extract herself from the chatty visitors' discussion. She informed them she could benefit from the "powder room" herself and wandered toward the house's back entrance, where the men had disappeared.

Mina's Interpol intelligence had issued her an internal blueprint of the home. Moving down a long, shadowed hallway, she could distinguish the two men conversing through the closed door of a library. Ensuring no one was about, she withdrew a tiny micro-transmitter from her clutch, then stooped and attached it to the door's base. Entering a vacant music room opposite the hallway, Mina sat in the first row of a dozen guest chairs and inserted the receiver into her ear. She was instantly privy to the private conversation behind the closed door across the hall.

"What kind of game are you playing here?" Tobias asked tersely. His eyes were wide with disbelief.

The two men stood in the mansion's library. Mabutu had taken his time surveying the room—oak tables, tall mahogany bookshelves. The French windows displayed a magnificent view across the outer lawns. He turned to his host. "I'm checking on your progress, my friend." He spoke without emotion. "Ensuring that our business arrangement has stabilized."

Tobias removed his tortoise-shell glasses and massaged the bridge of his nose. His left eyelid continued to twitch, and he opened a desk door and withdrew a small eyedrop bottle. Looking up at the high ceiling, he instilled two drops into his culprit left eye.

"You are not a natural criminal, Tobias," Mabutu said while feathering a smile. "After the incident last year, well . . ."

He referred to the sorry situation with Tobias' third victim: the college-age Vander Kellen girl. After drugging and securing the woman in his cul-de-sac hidey house, the female had become unhinged. By the third day of captivity, Crenshaw was forced to administer doses of ketamine—an animal tranquilizer—to keep her under control. Mabutu was correct. By nature, Tobias hadn't the stomach for indiscriminate violence. He was a scientist first and, admittedly, a kidnapper. He had called Mabutu for assistance, and the Liberian had dispensed his henchmen to deal with the situation.

After the spring thaw, the victim's body had washed ashore in Lake Michigan. It had been six months since she had initially disappeared. What had appeared to be a well-contrived financial arrangement at the time—Crenshaw capturing victims and Mabutu selling them—had shown the first signs of unraveling.

Mabutu now stepped to one of the windows and spoke without turning. "My Arab friends require another pair of victims."

"Impossible! That wasn't our arrangement."

"Arrangements change, don't they?"

Tobias considered how easily Mabutu's thugs had snuffed out the crazed female's life without a flinch of remorse. He stared across the room now at his old college chum. At last, he said, "Okay. I'll do it on one condition—this time, it's final."

The slickly garbed Mabutu turned from the window with a clipped smile. "Splendid," he said agreeably. "Upon delivery. Then we part our ways, and you're out for good."

Ten minutes later, after bidding farewell to Marla and other guests, Colonel Mabutu had hopped inside his rental Toyota and driven away down the mansion's curling driveway.

After his vehicle had vanished, Agent Mina Wilton slipped casually from the home's side exit, offering no goodbyes as she did the same. She followed Mabutu's exit via her tracking device, and her Saab tailed him at an unobservable distance. It was late afternoon, and she guessed the international flesh peddler was returning to his hotel.

While she tailed the crimson Toyota through the suburbs, Mina used the time to rehash her mission. The pieces were falling into place. Whether he realized it or not, the noose around Tazeki Mabutu's neck as an international trafficker was slowly tightening.

The conversation she'd just heard confirmed her theory. Mina now understood how Mabutu had procured his American targets. Tobias Crenshaw, his former college roommate, was the hunter of the victims. He'd employed some recipe of chemical sedation to execute the abductions. After gathering his victims and locking them drugged inside a secure location, the Colonel's men would arrive to transport the cargo to whatever the destination. Somewhere along the line, the captured females would be trained in their newfound careers as sex slaves, put up for sale or auction to whichever pervert was wealthy enough to purchase their services.

It was sick enough that Mina wanted to expel her lunch. But she dialed down her disgust by reminding herself that this was how their present world worked. No surprise. Humans have been enslaving one another since they were cave dwellers. While disgusting at its core, Mina rationalized that at least she was doing her small part to put the slimy bastards in prison where they belonged—hopefully until their dark souls rotted.

Her thoughts turned to the new player in the game: Tobias Crenshaw. The intelligence briefs had referred to him as an "unknown suspect." Possibly working as a.k.a. "the Chemist." She had previously communicated with the local Green Bay Police Department. She discovered their Special Crimes unit had worked on a string of local female disappearances, where six college-age victims had seemingly vanished into thin air. Except for one, Mina knew. A thirty-two-year-old named Maggie Jeffers was the fiancé of the lead detective in the case—Lt. Cale Van Waring. Mina had contacted Ms. Jeffers two days earlier (posing as a reporter) to get a feel for what the lady had gone through. And if she might be able to identify her abductor. Ms. Jeffers refused to comment and hung up. Mina, of course, hadn't known about Tobias Crenshaw then. But now, after eavesdropping on the conversation between Col. Mabutu and Crenshaw, new facts helped illuminate the puzzle. Perhaps Maggie Jeffers would reconsider talking to her after all.

Mina reached for her mobile phone, merging into traffic onto a bridge crossing the wide Fox River.

Mina parked the Saab in the shade of a strip mall lot, which stood adjacent to the more considerable lot reserved for hotel occupants. She watched the Colonel exit his rented Toyota. As Mabutu entered the Kress Inn's main doors, the young parking valet drove the vehicle away.

Mina pressed one of her phone apps. This activated the compact audio-video device she had planted in his hotel suite the night before when Mabutu had vacated for dinner. The device was activated now, displaying a trio of vacant rooms. The bug was disguised as a button in a padded armchair opposite the wide bedroom doors, where she could easily see the bed and a pair of matching dressers. The device also allowed her zoom capabilities via her phone app.

Mina scanned the suite. The room was first-rate all the way. New carpeting, private gas fireplace, computer modems with wireless Internet access, and a small kitchenette. All the amenities.

She watched now as Mabutu entered the suite and disappeared into the bathroom. He emerged minutes later wearing a purple kimono, and from a bedroom dresser drawer, he withdrew a large bundle wrapped in sand-toned oilcloth. He unwrapped the object on the bed, exposing a fifteen-inch Buddha-like statue. He turned and set it upright atop one dresser. It appeared troll-like, as if fashioned over a century ago.

Mabutu sat on the edge of the king-size mattress. His eyes scanned a city map, and he logged a GPS destination into his phone. Setting the items aside, he rose and lit a small incense bowl, which he'd placed atop the dresser beside the statue. He knelt upon the plush, plum-colored carpet and bowed his head, reciting a string of well-practiced incantations.

Fifteen minutes later, he rose and picked up the statue gently. He wrapped it back inside the oilcloth, then slipped the object inside a cardboard box he'd produced from one closet. With the sacred idol secure again, he slid the box back under the bed.

His ceremony complete, Mabutu disappeared into his bathroom once more. Mina extinguished the bugging device. She sat for minutes pondering what the bizarre ritual had meant. Likely some African religious thing. She shrugged, thinking, *to each his own*. Mina shifted the Saab into gear, exited the hotel parking lot, and headed back to her hotel eight blocks away.

~

It was the Saturday dinner hour. Chloe Jeffers swung into the left turn lane on Main Street with a glance in her rearview mirror. She frowned while peering into the side mirror, and with her right hand, she turned down the radio.

From the passenger seat, her sister, Maggie, gave her a questioning look. "Something the matter?"

"Just because you're not a secret agent," Chloe said cryptically, "doesn't mean you're not being followed."

The sun remained strong in the western sky. They were headed to St. Phillip's for the six o'clock mass. Maggie gazed out her passenger window while Chloe studied the rearview mirror. "A white Saab's been following us for the last six blocks." Chloe glanced at her sister. "Any ideas?"

Maggie started to turn, causing her sister to bark, "Don't! Keep looking straight ahead."

Maggie froze. You're either crazy or paranoid."

Chloe navigated through an intersection. "How about both?"

The Saab remained on their tail three car-lengths behind.

Moments later, the tall church steeple appeared between the rooftops of surrounding homes, and the sisters discerned the structure's solid gray brick. The parking lot was half-filled. They had time to slip inside and have their sins washed away in confession before the official service commenced.

Chloe turned left at the first corner ahead and parked the Buick in the shade of a gnarled ash tree. She watched the Saab park in the lot across the street behind them. A slender, thirty-ish blonde emerged, not even glancing their way. The woman wore dressy jeans and a sleeveless summer blouse. She was phone texting as she strode toward the church.

Chloe chided herself. Maybe Maggie was right. Perhaps she was being over-paranoid—if such a thing existed.

The sisters moved across the street. A handful of other parishioners ahead of them advanced toward the wide front entrance.

"The confession line might be long," Maggie suggested. "We're early enough." Chloe walked a half-step ahead. "Besides, Ed's inside saving us seats."

As they neared the church's broad front steps, the blonde with the cell phone had stopped and lingered ahead, still texting. As they approached her, the lady abruptly turned to them with a smile.

"Hello, Maggie. I'm Mina Wilton," the woman said calmly. "We spoke on the phone the other day. I've got added information on your kidnapper—"

"You're the one who's been bothering her," Chloe jumped in, her displeasure undisguised.

The lady ignored her, speaking directly to Maggie. "I'm an Interpol agent. I want to ask you—"

"Sure you are," interrupted Chloe. "And I'm the Easter Bunny."

Mina said, "Look. I'm serious about talking to—"

Chloe reached out and slapped the iPhone from the lady's hand, knocking it to the sidewalk. It skidded across the cement and landed face-down in the gutter.

"Are you insane?" Mina asked wildly. "Why did you—"

"This isn't a freak show, lady." Chloe's voice was stern. "Next time, make an appointment."

Steering Maggie by the elbow, they marched past the open-mouth lady and climbed the church's front steps. They disappeared into the comfortable inner shadows. When confessing her indiscretions, Chloe would add another sin or two to the list.

Departing from the hotel around six p.m., Tazeki Mabutu drove his rental car across town. He headed to a suburb about fifteen minutes away. Reaching his destination, he parked the Toyota two blocks up the street, tucked beneath shade trees. Exiting, he walked up the block in his dark green jogging suit, unhurriedly, intent on blending in. He carried a mid-sized duffle bag and scanned the area. Birds chirped from above, and he detected charcoal in the calm evening air.

Crossing a quiet intersection, Mabutu examined the suburban neighborhood. A kid was riding a bike down the block, and beyond him, a man hosed an SUV in his driveway. It was doubtful anyone would question Mabutu's presence in his jogger disguise, but if so, he'd limp in discomfort and confess to a leg cramp. He had no explanation for the duffle bag and doubted he'd need one.

A pleasant suburban neighborhood at dinnertime on a Saturday evening. No one paid the slightest attention as Mabutu reached his destination. There, he veered off the sidewalk and disappeared between thick juniper bushes. He entered the open side lawn of the Van Waring property, approaching from the west.

It took Mabutu twenty minutes to study the property's angles and survey the trees, bushes, shrubs, and every nook, mound, and ditch. He even waved in a window at a cat staring out. At last, he located a prime position for his purpose—an open space tucked inside a cluster of high bushes just past the garages along the lot's eastern border. He disappeared inside the glade, which extended about twenty yards along the property line. Hidden by bushes and trees, he gazed out across the expansive lawn. He spied a robin's nest in a chestnut tree, with two crows searching the ground beneath it.

Mabutu removed a dozen charms and paraphernalia from his duffle. He knelt on the ground and closed his eyes, envisioning the territory around him. Next, he employed the charms to cast a repellent spell that dissuaded animals and humans from approaching his enclosure. One crow sensed the magical activity and cawed loudly as it lifted ahead of the spell's clawing fingers. The second crow was not as fortunate. It shuddered and rolled sideways on the lawn, legs kicking before it expired.

Inside the thicket, Mabutu stared out at the lawns and flower beds of Detective Cale Van Waring's residence. The avian and rodent activity within the property's borders had ceased like turning off a spigot. Yes, she smiled. The hidden space would serve his purposes. He now needed fresh blood to perform his ritual—preferably human.

Mina's Saab cruised up the street past the Van Waring residence. She was frustrated by what had happened outside the church. She was hardly any stalker or nut case but an undercover Interpol agent trying to unravel a human trafficking case.

Picturing Maggie's sister, Mina shook her head. Now, there was one rude-crude woman. She had only needed three quick questions answered by Maggie, recorded on her phone. How innocent could that be?

Instead, Ms. Rude-Crude had slapped her mobile away as if Mina were some two-bit paparazzi. How embarrassing. *And outside a church, no less.* Her phone was ruined, and Mina considered sending Ms. Rude-Crude the replacement bill.

She still had her digital recorder in the glove box. It would suffice. On the drive to Maggie's residence, Mina promised herself she wouldn't retreat to her hotel room like a scolded puppy. She had failed twice now at conversing with Ms. Jeffers. *The third time's the charm.* Mina knew persistence was vital to locking criminals and perverts behind bars. Would Maggie Jeffers recognize Tobias Crenshaw as her kidnapper? It was a simple question that Mina needed to know.

She decided to wait for Maggie's return home from church services—alone this time. Mina guessed Maggie might be equally embarrassed by her sister's behavior and concede to answer questions about her husband's investigation, her kidnapping, and her (Mina's) theory about where the other kidnapped victims might be.

Mina studied the neighborhood where she sat parked. The homes were pleasant and spaced comfortably apart, easily double the standard American lot size. Mature trees and bushes isolated many of the houses. The layout worked to Mina's advantage. She'd approach Maggie's front door without appearing as a threat.

Mina now spotted a slender man in jogging attire as he emerged up the block from a cluster of trees. The man seemed to ignore her vehicle while at the same time studying it. He veered across the street at mid-block and headed in her direction. Mina tensed, suddenly recognizing the figure. Despite the costume change, it was Colonel Mabutu—soldier, diplomat, and suspected human trafficker. The dossier had further informed Mina that he was Liberia's most accomplished voodoo master—a powerful *bokor*—a witch priest. Interpol, however, brushed aside this part of Mabutu's resume. The agency consisted of spies and intelligence-gathering agents. They were hardly interested in witch-hunting.

Mina eyed her clutch on the passenger seat. It concealed her small Sig automatic. She could get to the loaded weapon in two seconds if necessary.

The disguised jogger motioned her to roll down the window as he neared her vehicle. Mina complied, playing along, curious at knowing his game at the detective's residence.

"Saabs are excellent vehicles. Great gas mileage." The jogger's smile was phony, and in a different outfit herself, Mina doubted he'd recognize her from the afternoon party. She seldom dressed to stand out. So here she was, just an everyday slacks-and-sweater gal in a quiet neighborhood.

She Americanized her accent. "You betcha. We love it." Confirming that she was not on her own.

"Very Euro." The jogger kept his grin in place, moving across the patch of lawn nearer the vehicle. Mina watched as he slipped his hand into his jacket pocket and leaned closer to her open window.

She remained frozen, desiring not to spook the visitor. "Do you live around here?" she inquired.

Mabutu withdrew his hand, lifting it to his lips. Before Mina guessed what was happening, he blew on his fingers, widening them like a stage magician while releasing a powdery substance.

Alarm bells clanged in her head, propelling her away from the open window. Confined by her seatbelt, Mina fumbled for the window controls—missing the button twice while attempting to close it. It slowly buzzed up at last, but too late. Greasy gray shadows gathered inside the vehicle's confined space, clutching at her throat with ghoulish fingers. She cried out in a rasping voice, watching the late-day sunlight turn dull and blotchy.

Moments later, Mina heard her final sound as her head thumped softly against the window.

By 7:40, the sun was lowering, and the western horizon was bathed in a chartreuse glow.

Pulling up the driveway and returning home, Maggie and Chloe screamed together in shock. A bird of some kind—a crow, from the looks of it—was nailed to Maggie's backdoor. Below it sat a sealed cardboard box on the steps, which they were leery of touching. In a panic, Maggie phoned Cale's partner, Detective Slink Dooley. With her voice shaking, she reported the bizarre situation at her home.

Maggie knew Slink was free on Saturday evenings. It took only five minutes for him to arrive at his best friend's house. Exiting in jeans and a polo shirt, Slink stood wide-eyed as the sisters extracted the deceased fowl from the door. They dropped it in a dark plastic trash bag, unable to disguise their disgust. Chloe secured the bag and deposited it inside a garbage container in the garage. Slink observed them as they bleach-cleaned the door and back porch steps.

Slink said, "They should give you guys a neighborhood cleaning award."

Chloe was unamused. "I wonder who my sister here PO'd."

"I'm an attorney, remember?" Maggie countered. She shifted her attention to the cardboard box, studying the return label. It was addressed to them from Italy, with Cale's signature on the return. "Back in law school, they told us we would make enemies."

"Same thing for cops," Slink shrugged knowingly. "You don't join the force to make friends."

"Hello? A dead bird tacked to your door?" Chloe narrowed her eyes at them. "Luckily, we never got those warnings in beauty college."

Minutes later, having placed the two-foot square box on the kitchen counter, they watched as Chloe bravely opened the flaps. She withdrew a wrapped, fifteen-inch Buddha-like statue. Maggie's eyes widened, standing next to Slink, who muttered, "What the hell?" He immediately suspected that Cale had sent the package as a gag. Tomorrow was his birthday—an event Cale despised—and Slink guessed his partner had sent the statue to jokingly warn them against taking the event too seriously. The return address from Italy was the punchline, Slink decided. Regardless of why Cale had sent it, the statue set Chloe off. She dropped the ceramic idol back into the box as if it had burned her hands.

Chloe set off across the kitchen and dining room, pacing back and forth. She barked loudly about demons, possessions, and ancient dark spirits, frowning the whole time. Back in the kitchen again, she rooted through the pantry for several items. Then Chloe sped back to the open archway separating the dining and living rooms. Slink and Maggie both watched her performance wide-eyed.

"Looks like somebody missed their afternoon nap," Slink offered up.

Staring at her sister, Maggie shouted, "Chloe! Stop it right now!" Chloe glanced over at them with half-crazed eyes. Maggie added, "What's going on with you?"

Chloe had dropped to her knees inside the open area of the living room. Ignoring Maggie, she drew a large chalk circle on the hardwood floor. Rising, she stepped back to the box and withdrew the fifteen-inch statue. Over at the circle once more, Chloe placed it upright inside. This done, she grabbed a large Morton's salt container and poured a white ring around the circle's circumference.

"For protection," she explained to them without looking up. With these tasks accomplished, she stepped back and surveyed her artistry.

Maggie studied her sister with her jaw clenched. "What in the world—"

"I told you," Chloe repeated. "For protection."

"From what?" Slink asked, confused. "A crazy little gnome figurine?" He smirked. "Or whatever it is?"

Slink opened the refrigerator and withdrew a beer bottle. Opening it, he swallowed while shifting his gaze between both ladies. He was off duty, but this Saturday evening performance topped anything he'd be watching on cable.

After finishing her bizarre task, Chloe gathered the items of her project and stepped back into the dining room. She studied the upright statue in the circle on the living room floor.

"Care to tell us what that was all about?" Maggie asked pointedly.

Ten minutes later, Chloe had explained to them about African voodoo and demonic possession and how seemingly innocent items called fetishes or "*bocio*" could be super-charged with curses—the stuff of otherworld influences or activities.

"Some kids nailed a dead bird to our door, Chlo," Maggie scowled. "And you go voodoo bonkers?"

Chloe slipped past them to the refrigerator. Grabbing a beer for herself, she opened it and gulped four long glugs before turning back to them. She snarked, "Have you forgotten I'm a psychic?"

"Cale sent it to us from Italy." Maggie retorted. "He's in Chicago, so it must be some joke."

"His taste in sculpture seems seriously lacking." Slink finished his beer and set the empty in the sink.

"Believe what you want," Chloe said. "I'm taking no chances with that . . . *thing*."

Outside, twilight had surrendered to the dark, and the driveway security lights near the garages were aglow. Slink glanced at his watch. "Gotta run, kids." He stepped toward the backdoor. "I predict my evening will be saner from here on out." With an eye-roll from Chloe, he stepped outside.

Maggie leaned halfway out the door, calling to him, "Thanks for coming over. Sorry if we seemed frazzled."

They could hear thumping sounds in the distance, like a graduation party in gear blocks away.

Slink shot her a thumbs-up and strode across the well-lit apron. His Taurus stood parked in the darker shadows, a car length behind Chloe's Buick. He called back over his shoulder, "If Chloe needs to visit the psych ward, call 911—not me."

With a smile, Maggie dipped back into the house. At the kitchen window, Chloe pulled the curtain aside and watched Slink's lean figure slip into the driveway shadows, which blanketed his dark gray vehicle like a funeral shroud.

The night was in full force as Slink withdrew his car keys. Behind him, the lights were ablaze, and he studied the house and surrounding yard for a long moment. All seemed in order except for the thumping of the distant party noise. Slink guessed the racket would end before 10 p.m. It was nothing anyone living in the suburbs hadn't heard a hundred times before.

Despite Chloe's odd behavior, he decided that his five-block trip over had been a waste of time. Other than a potential animal cruelty charge, no crime had been committed. Both sisters were safe inside, which was why he'd responded to Maggie's harried phone call in the first place—the chance of a threat.

Slink understood Cale's flight would arrive home in an hour or so. Cale had flown to Chicago two days ago for a meeting with a pair of FBI agents assisting them on their kidnapping case. The suspicion was that it might involve overseas sex trafficking, as well.

His partner had cabbed it to the airport two days earlier and would do so coming home. What Slink couldn't understand was Cale's sending that cardboard box addressed from Italy—of all places. It made little sense. And especially with that insane Buddha statue tucked inside. The crazy episode had triggered Chloe, and the humor of it now made Slink grin. It was undoubtedly a prank Cale had dreamed up, and Slink guessed his partner would be laughing his ass off all the way home from Chicago.

No sounds whispered from inside the Van Waring house. Yet outside, the low, persistent thumping of the hollow log drums and shakers continued. The voodoo priest had summoned the drums, and they opened the gateways for his calling down of the ancestral spirits. The invisible veil had been opened.

Tucked within the jumble of tall bushes at the property's edge, Mabutu was now in full witch-doctor mode. Painted white ringlets encircled his eyes, and matching streaks clawed each side of his face. More zig-zag paint streams ran down his smooth, ebony torso. He knelt before his makeshift altar tableau on the ground inside the tree stand. His hex had been cast out to the property's far edges, and an invisible bubble encapsulated all within. The heady backbeat of the skin drums had replaced the nightly cricket chorus, thrumming through the charged evening air. The sounds of his spell filled the atmosphere, as soft or loud as the *bokor* commanded.

Raising his head, he called upon Papa Legba to open the doors of the Netherworld. To call down the loa that he sought. Through the intercession of Matre Kalfu, Mabutu expressed his desire for a sinister *Baka* spirit to assist him. He summoned the bitter loa in its form as a hefty, eight-foot-long green serpent.

Despite the persistent drumming, Mabutu was alert to foreign noises or movements in the darkness. Fifteen feet away from him, the unblinking eyes of the bodiless blonde's head—elevated on a three-foot high pike—watched the man in the polo shirt emerge from the house's backdoor. The man moved toward the pair of vehicles parked on the driveway's concrete apron, just beyond in the glow of the annoying flood lights.

Mabutu watched and waited.

Mina stared out at the backyard, only able to shift her eyes back and forth. Her neckless head was stuck in place. She was entirely under the witch doctor's control. Though she had no torso or limbs, her open eyes peered across the backyard with interest.

Mina watched the man cross the driveway toward his parked sedan. The jungle drums, aided by bells and shakers, continued to thump, defying at least a dozen noise ordinances. Yet the man seemed unconcerned. Mina wished she could warn him of the insane voodoo monster lurking nearby, but she had no arms to wave or vocal cords to shout with. She could only blink her eyes and watch.

As he neared his Taurus, Slink stopped. He felt an icy tremor of premonition slide up his spine—his detective's instinct. He considered returning to the house, remaining on guard until Cale arrived home from the airport. But common sense bested him, and Slink decided the idea was silly, especially with Chloe behaving as if she'd swallowed a half-dozen bennies. A witch's circle drawn on the floor? Morton's salt? With the little Buddha statue trapped inside it like Hannibal Lecter?

Perhaps Chloe had been sniffing too many perm fumes at the beauty salon where she worked.

The thumping drums continued their low pounding. Curiously, Slink felt drawn toward the cluster of high bushes beyond the edge of the garages. The thumping drums continued from down the block, and the low clouds echoed them in the night. Kids were having a grad party or birthday bash, Slink decided. With his senses on high alert, the summer air smelled sweet. And the shady side lawn continued summoning him like a siren luring sailors toward the rocks. Slink suddenly felt oddly compelled to examine the bushes and tall trees opposite the driveway.

Standing near his car, he considered Chloe's odd behavior. And why had a slaughtered crow been tacked to the home's backdoor? Something strange was a-foot tonight, and an abnormal aura seemed to hang low over the neighborhood. Slink felt his neck hairs rise.

Considering his weapon holstered in the glove box, he shrugged away his paranoia. After all, he was at his best friend's house on a Saturday night. Slink again studied the shadowy side lawn beyond the garages. Something about the bushes was pulling him that way. He decided *what the hell*, throwing caution to the wind, and stepped toward the pitch-black area. The sweet odor of jasmine was more pungent here, and the drums more intense. As he neared the spot, Slink noticed tiny fireflies flickering deep inside the bushes. As his eyes adjusted to the shadows, he spotted the vague form of what appeared to be a girl's head sitting pegged atop a high stick.

Slink's body jerked as something landed heavily on his back. It clung to his neck and shoulders like an invisible weight. His muscles spasmed, and his face contorted. His arms and legs went rigid, and his body lurched and staggered. He lumbered forward into the thick black bushes like a man walking mindlessly into a forest.

Then Slink Dooley felt Nothing.

Mabutu slipped from the bush thicket, the elm branches swaying above in the night breeze. He ramped the drumbeats up a level and sized up the *nzambi* he had created. With the invisible loa riding the man's back, his face appeared like the Baka serpent. The voodoo priest smirked and strode across the grass. He kept within the shadows, away from the security lights. The zombie trailed behind him, moving with the dead-legged gait of a tranquilized orangutan.

Mabutu glanced over his shoulder at Mina's head on its wooden spike. Her ardent green eyes were transfixed on him. At the parked Taurus, he fobbed open the door and leaned inside. He fished out the .38-caliber service revolver from the glove box before closing the door soundlessly.

Handing the weapon to the zombie, Mabutu led the way across the lawn, silently moving around the shady side of the house. The skin drums pounded in rhythm to their steps, and the butter-eyed moon stared down on them beneath a canopy of stars and smoky clouds.

From her perch atop the stake in the lawn, Mina's disembodied head listened to the guttural pulse of the drums. She no longer cared about anything except watching the events unfold—a meager form of entertainment. As she eyed the ebony lawn along the house's side, sparse lights glowed around the window's edge as if the occupants inside might be watching television.

White candles flickered around the protective salt circle. Standing in the dining room ten feet away, Chloe crossed her arms and stared at the demonic little Buddha statue. It glowed faintly orange from deep within. Hearing the thumping drum sounds outside still, she stepped further into the living room and eased the drapes aside. She peeked out into the darkness alongside the house. Nothing. The far-off, dull percussion sounded like a gangsta SUV cruising through the nighttime streets.

"What's that racket?" Maggie asked, emerging from the bathroom. "Did you turn on the TV?"

"It's from outside someplace." Chloe released the curtains and watched her sister open the refrigerator door. "Haven't you had enough wine, Mags?" Chloe asked judgmentally. "You're pregnant, in case you forgot."

"That Swedish study." Maggie countered. "A couple of nips are healthy. It's the flavonoids."

Chloe was in no mood to argue. Besides, who was she to talk? She believed in magic, hexes, psychic visions, and voodoo spells. And yes, in witch's circles. Only a minute ago, she heard a strange voice in her head warning: *They are coming!*

Great, Chloe thought. Just what we need on top of everything else tonight.

She decided to keep her snarky comments to herself. Thanks to the glowing Buddha idol and dead bird nailed to the door, Maggie was edgy enough tonight. It wasn't wise to push her sister's buttons.

Smart move, Chlo, her inner voice chided. Keep your fat trap shut.

Across in the kitchen, Maggie held a glass of merlot in one hand. "Besides," she said, "I thought we were celebrating Cale's return tonight?"

Chloe almost took the bait but bit her tongue. She asked herself: *Why am I so jumpy? What's going on here tonight?* She watched Maggie take another sip of wine while standing in the kitchen with her elbows on the countertop. Chloe understood her sister was under *mucho* pressure lately. And her stress level would shoot through the roof if the paternity test she'd taken proved that her rapist was the baby's father instead of Cale.

Maggie said, "Why don't you put some music on? Drown out that stupid pounding?"

"Quiet helps me think."

"You call pounding drums quiet?"

Chloe gazed down at the evil little statue. Had Cale honestly sent it to them from Italy? It made no sense to her. Yet there was no denying it—the diminutive Buddha seemed to be changing. Chloe wondered if it was simply a reflection of the surrounding flickering candles. No. She was sure the statue was taking on an orange inner glow.

She watched the Buddha's smug expression twist into a more sinister sneer. Chloe's inner voice cautioned: *Keep it together, Chlo. Now's not the time for your imagination to start spinning cartwheels.*

As a taxi entered the driveway, Mina stared curiously into the night from her tall pike amid the bushes. Its tires rolled up the weathered gray concrete until the vehicle stopped behind Slink's car, three-quarters up the drive.

From the backseat, Cale eyed Slink's Taurus in the headlight glare. Ahead of it on the apron stood Chloe's Buick. He knew his and Maggie's vehicles would be tucked safely inside the garages.

Cale stared out the cab's side window. The security lights glowed across the lawn, but dark pockets of shadow lurked closer to the house. The inside was illuminated faintly, the light behind the closed dining room blinds barely detectable. Cale heard distant thumping sounds, and for one panicky moment, it reminded him of jungle drums. His thoughts flashed back to Liberia, where he had nearly lost his life at the hands of a psychotic witch doctor named Mabutu. Cale shook away the memory, but the thumping persisted. Was it coming from inside the house? Maybe from the stereo? Or some graduation party up the block?

Whatever the case, Cale's inner gut warned him: *Something isn't right.*

His watch said 9:34 p.m. Why hadn't the neighbors complained? He damn sure would have. Cale was surprised patrol units weren't parked outside, with uniforms rapping on the doors. Then again, it was a warm Saturday night. Maybe people shrugged off things they would have complained about in the past, desiring not to deal with the hassle.

He'd find out if it came from his house in a minute.

Cale carried no luggage from his short flight home from Chicago. As tired as he was, he'd almost forgotten that tomorrow was his birthday. After watching the cabby reverse down the driveway, he strode to the backdoor. The thumping sound grew louder—no doubt it was coming from inside. Cale steeled himself as he keyed the lock. His jaw tightened, prepared to grin like an idiot when they all leaped out shouting:

"Surprise!"

Mina, silent and serene, watched emotionlessly as the events around her unfolded. Her eyes could almost see around the half-open curtain of one side window. Her brain, however, allowed her to imagine what unhealthy events might already be unfolding within.

In the initial zombie attack, a large potted rubber plant had toppled along with two dining room chairs. Crusty mulch sprayed over both men, and Cale spat loam from his mouth while fighting off his attacking opponent. But Slink—now in zombified form—remained on top of him, punching, swinging, relentless. Cale could feel something hard poking against his rib cage as they grappled chest-to-chest on the dining room table. The object felt solid, and he guessed it was the butt of a handgun.

Cale swung his elbow, warding off his partner's crazed attack while hoping it smashed into Slink's cheekbone, chin, or eye. Hopefully, all three. He was trying to knock some sense into the guy, who was high on either PCP or meth, as near as Cale could guess.

"Slink! It's *me*, damn it! Cale!"

No response but for two strong hands encircling his throat. Cale twisted his head sideways, staring across the room at the half-naked voodoo nutjob who sat calmly in a living room armchair. His painted face only displayed a sardonic grimace, as if he cheered for neither man in this death match.

A distance away, Chloe knelt sobbing against a side wall. She was helplessly in shock, whimpering childlike, down on her knees not far from where the painted psycho invader sat.

"Stand down, you moron!" Cale grunted the command at Slink as they fought atop the wide table. "Slink! Are you . . . *crazy! Stand down, dammit!*"

The jungle drums' intensity increased, trapping both men inside the throbbing pulse of aggression. Slink had one knee pressed against Cale's groin, both hands struggling to secure Cale in a chokehold. Cale countered by keeping one arm slipped inside Slink's elbows, grabbing his wrists and forearms, forcing the pressure away.

While this happened, a panic-stricken Chloe rose and charged madly across the room toward the glowing Buddha statue. However, before she reached it, her body was lifted mid-air and propelled invisibly back across the room. The shattering glass *exploded* like a gunshot, slicing through the heavily charged atmosphere. An unseen force had propelled Chloe out the large side window, sending her flying like a heavy trash bag heaved onto a junk pile.

Despite the ringing in his ears, Cale felt Slink's hands tighten around his neck. Only this time, Cale's stamina and resistance were fading. He recalled his partner's words from weeks ago, when they'd discovered that the man who had kidnapped Maggie also raped her: *"I'll choke the last living breath out of the bastard,"* Slink had sworn bitterly.

Was his partner attempting that now? At the moment? Doing the same thing to Cale?

On the verge of letting go, he gazed beneath the room's arch, still baffled by the witch doctor's presence in his living room. While pondering the oddity, a poignant thought struck Cale—a revelation more significant than any he could recall:

I am staring at the embodiment of insanity.

The roaring blast of a gunshot rocked the room.

With Cale's fading vision fixed across the room on Mabutu, he watched as a dark smear exploded apart his left eye socket. The witch doctor flew backward like a man tossed from a horse. He crashed through a coffee table and did not move.

At that exact second, while staring at Mabutu's unbreathing carcass surrounded by glass on the wooden floor, Cale felt Slink's hands release his throat. As if a spell were broken, his partner dropped off the table to the floor like a puppet whose strings were snipped.

Across the opposite side of the room, Cale spied Maggie holding her 9mm automatic in the two-handed grip he'd taught her. She shifted her aim and blasted a second and third round downward, blowing a diminutive Buddha statue to pieces.

"Good shot, Mags," was all Cale could rasp before passing out cold.

From her unmoving station on the shadowy lawn, Mina watched the evening's dramatic aftermath.

Crime techs moved in and out of the house long into the night. Photos were snapped at multiple locations, inside and out. Despite the late hour, a crowd of neighbors gathered at the driveway base, their phones recording any activity beyond the long yellow crime scene tape.

Klieg lights focused on select lawn areas like a movie set whose final scenes had wrapped.

Across the side lawn, inside a thicket of high bushes at the property's edge, Cale watched Dr. Heinz Mocarek pronounce a headless female body as "deceased." The cause of death was recorded as a "Machete attack." Forensic techs had located the instrument's handle protruding from a nearby duffle bag.

Not far away, Cale observed the techs removing the female victim's head from its tall spike before gentling it into a transparent plastic evidence bag. The eyes appeared half-open and seemed to blink moments later. Likely due to gravity, he imagined.

"Involuntary ocular muscle spasms," the M.E. informed Cale, who watched with morbid curiosity as the severed head was bagged. "French physicians verified it centuries ago," the doctor added. His grisly tasks were complete, and he was packing up. "Severed heads would blink up to ten minutes after being guillotined. Even try conversing, according to some reports."

Cale eyed the doctor as if awaiting a punchline.

"Some neurologists postulate that thoughts might remain up to ten minutes after death." The doctor shrugged nonchalantly.

"Creepy," was Cale's response.

Stepping across the driveway behind them, a uniformed officer approached. He informed Cale that officers had discovered a rental Saab parked a half-block up the street. Paperwork showed it rented by one Mina Wilton. A British passport. Age thirty-nine." He eyed Cale. "And you're not going to believe this, Lieutenant."

"I'd believe just about anything right now."

"Her ID says she's an Interpol Agent."

The silence expanded as they processed how the revelation fit into the crime scene's convoluted puzzle. Dr. Mocarek remained practical. "We'll photograph her face. Send it with her fingerprints to Interpol's NCB lab for confirmation."

Cale nodded solemnly. He turned and walked back toward his house after informing the doctor they'd talk more tomorrow. He still had statements to give the detectives inside.

Cale and Slink—in separate rooms—conveyed their stories to state homicide investigators, who admitted they'd never seen anything close to the bizarreness of this crime scene. Chloe required treatment for multiple glass lacerations but suffered Nothing worse than a sprained shoulder. Maggie was in shock, and her pregnancy became an immediate concern to the paramedics. Cale kept his thoughts to himself, looking like he'd been in an alley brawl with the local Hell's Angels chapter. And though bruised about his face and neck, Slink Dooley confessed that he recalled little since departing Cale's house earlier in the evening.

At the paramedics' request, Maggie was spared aggressive questioning about the home invasion. No matter how you sliced it, the investigators understood that the paperwork alone would take until daybreak to complete.

Slink and Chloe were driven to their homes by patrol cruisers. They'd rest in their own beds tonight, imagining when waking that they'd dreamt the entire peculiar affair. Despite Mabutu's corpse being transported away by the meat wagon, Cale and Maggie declined Chloe's offer of spending the night in her spare bedroom. Instead, they'd grab a few hours of sleep (if possible) in a hotel only a mile away.

The sisters hugged and promised they'd talk tomorrow once the shock had worn off,

Thanking the officer for the lift to the Drift Inn, Cale and Maggie walked toward the lighted front entrance. Each carried a small overnight bag, and the "Vacancy" sign behind them cast their approach in long shadows.

Maggie finally asked, "So, other than the past two hours, how was your trip?"

"Uneventful, for the most part," Cale replied drily. "Until Slink attacked me for running out of beer—if I had to guess."

Their weak smiles faded as they entered the front doors. They hesitated to appear to the front desk clerk like Saturday night stoners wandering in off the street.

Scattered thoughts flitted through Mina's head, the way tiny birds dart between tree branches. These glimpses were semi-lucid, and she had trouble deciding whether she was deceased or locked in some Kafkaesque dream. If she were honestly "gone to her maker," as her mother used to say at funerals, was it possible that Mina was trapped in an in-between place like Purgatory? Which she had been taught was a type of "holding cell" for souls awaiting final judgment.

Rather than ponder the unknown, Mina focused on what was happening around her. She concentrated on the drone of massive engines on both sides of what might be an aircraft. The idea allowed her to meld things into some coherence, for whatever it was worth.

The closest she had felt to her former self was when some lab technician had stitched Mina's head back atop her dislocated body. They had then placed her inside a coolant-infused coffin, ready for transport back to her family in the U.K. She imagined they'd embalm her there after landing in preparation for a proper Christian burial.

It all made sense to Mina's analytical way of thinking.

One major flaw in her logic remained: how did she understand what was happening? And how could she envision what was going on around her? Might it have something to do with the existence of her soul?

Mina contemplated these strange thoughts while the plane had lifted off and settled into a cruising altitude. She was somewhere (she guessed) over the Atlantic Ocean. Assuming further that she wasn't locked in a mental institution somewhere, hallucinating everything, it left Mina with an intriguing predicament.

She felt herself pale when recalling her ordeal. *Hexes, spells, and voodoo witch doctors turning people into mindless slaves or zombies.* She felt trapped in an intricate web. Yet, as things stood, Mina considered her possibilities moving forward. If not drugged or comatose, could she be part of a complex AI computer simulation? And if not, was there a chance she might eventually become a *zombie*? Half-alive, half-dead? Imprisoned between human and un-human?

Mina lay rigid in her transport coffin, unable to quiet these galloping thoughts. She had been tasked with apprehending the Liberian Colonel Tazeki Mabutu, a known sex trafficker, sadist, and voodoo priest. A powerful *bokor*.

She recalled inhaling the powder he'd blown into the open window of her rented Saab. One of the traditional hallmarks of Petra voodoo was the turning of living people into obedient zombies. Yet here she was, lucidly contemplating her fate. Situationally aware, as it were. And such being the case, did that not make her less of a mindless lifeform and more of *something else*?

Mina admitted that this was not the end she had envisioned for herself. And even more puzzling, how could she exist as a *zombie* without being controlled by a master? Or mistress? Wasn't that the rule? To submit to whatever commands they ordered? And void of someone issuing her rudimentary directions from here on out, wouldn't she fade into energy-less nonexistence? The way a motor vehicle cannot function without a battery?

Regardless of all this, the most confounding question of all rose in Mina's troubled mind as she felt the airplane now beginning its descent:

What next?

Almost Died Event # 6 – FATAL BOTTLE ROCKET – age 18

It was a post-graduation party, and we were all drunk. It was at the corner house on Monroe Street. Earlier, I threw empty beer bottles like a knife thrower, crashing four bottles near Hank's head. We laughed like fools. In the driveway later, Baglip backed his El Camino up before the garage doors. He and others fired bottle rockets off the open back at us. I charged them with raised arms like a lineman blocking a field goal. A fiery dart slammed into my left arm, inches from my eye. My arm bled like a SOB. Without it raised, the dart through my eyeball would have entered my brain and killed me. We continued drinking beer all night.

THE DECOY

Logline: A pair of detectives staking-out a potential serial kidnapper are surprised when the psychopath turns the tables and captures the female investigator instead.

The spacious Lumber Liquidators parking lot was half-filled with cars, vans, and SUVs. Detective Rita LaCosta sat in her Toyota, watching a few tiny raindrops tease her windshield. No need to even flip the wipers. She glanced across the parking lot at the front doors, watching several customers enter and exit. A half-minute later, she spoke into the com-transmitter fastened to the collar of her warmup jacket.

"You got eyes on, Stretcher?"

The voice came back in her ear. "Twenty-twenty. Are you sure you're ready for this?"

"My middle name," Rita said, glancing behind her through the rearview mirror. "I can't make you. You in some pimp ride from Compound?"

"I'm invisible—like we agreed. That's the point, right?"

Rita felt vulnerable, knowing her backup was somewhere nearby yet invisible. She continued studying the damp parking lot and the variety of moving people. The earlier mild drizzle had stopped, and perhaps fifty or so parked vehicles were now present. The "God's Gift" abductor was waiting out there somewhere. If all went as planned and their confidential informant's information proved correct, they'd spring the trap and arrest the bastard. Have the sick pervert in custody and, hopefully, processed by lunchtime.

"We got a trigger word yet?" Rita asked.

"'Haymaker,'" Stretcher said in her ear. "You call it out, and I'm there in twelve seconds."

"Gotcha." She reached for the door handle. "I'm exiting now."

"Remember, LaCosta," his voice encouraged, "you're the windshield, not the bug."

"Roger that." Rita smiled. "You need to work on your rah-rah speech, Detective." She heard his chuckle as she opened her car door.

God's Gift watched from a distance. The attractive late-20s female exited an older red Honda Civic and walked toward the lumber store's entrance. She wore workout leggings and a warmup top. Her blond hair was ponytailed, and her white cross-trainers stepped across the damp pavement. He calculated that she would not be inside for long from her gait and demeanor.

A worn leather Gucci bag sat on the van's passenger seat, and he separated the flaps and withdrew a squeezable plastic bottle filled with clear liquid. The bottle read "Skin Moisturizer."

Gazing out the windows, checking all directions, he exited his blue van. He was a picture of calm as he strolled around checking make-believe tire pressures. He wore black jeans and a dark navy peacoat with the collar turned up against the cool spring breeze. His ballcap was dipped low. Thin lambskin gloves covered God's Gift's hands. No actor in Hollywood could have feigned interest in Goodyear Polytreads with greater aplomb. From the corner of his eye, he watched a handful of people dodge lingering puddles as they moved to-and-from the store's front entrance. As far as they were concerned, he was invisible.

Wandering from the van, he slipped between the rows of parked cars. He sidestepped a pickup's bumper and a wayward shopping cart. Nearing the Toyota, he withdrew the plastic bottle from his pocket and, passing by, coated the driver's door handle with clear, slightly viscous fluid.

Back in his van seconds later, he could barely keep his heart from galloping. His forehead was damp near the hairline, and his shirt clammy along his lower back. The trap was set. It was time to sit and wait.

Breezing through the exit doors ten minutes later, Rita strode across the parking lot with a small shopping bag in one hand. She fished the keys from her warmup pocket, popped the Civic's locks, grabbed the door handle, and opened it. The handle was slick with what she guessed was mist or rainwater. Some clear fluid. She rubbed her fingertips together and sniffed them—slightly more viscous than rain-mist. Odorless. She wiped the dampness on the hem of her warmup, deciding it shouldn't stain.

A car cruised slowly up the far opposite lane. She wondered if it was Stretcher, perhaps changing to a different spot. Rita slipped inside her vehicle, closed the door, and placed the bag on the passenger seat. She fumbled with her keys while glancing in her rearview mirror. Someone in a blue van had parked behind her, blocking her from backing out. Rita sighed. She slid her key into the ignition without turning it. A glance in the rearview showed the unmoving vehicle still paused, perhaps waiting for an open slot ahead. Or maybe it was a shopper with a full cart or a mom pushing a baby stroller. She couldn't discern what was holding up the blue van from blocking her exit.

Turning her head, Rita wondered if the sudden blockage might be deliberate. Their CI had informed them God's Gift's MO was to park his victims in so they could not escape. Stretcher was watching all this, Rita knew. As if reading her mind, she heard his coms voice in her ear:

"Stay calm. Don't get your undies in a twist."

She knew Stretcher—wherever he was—had it covered. She knew he had her back, and she was okay.

The van remained stagnant. Rita considered bleating her horn, but Stretcher's words still lingered. She told herself to relax. Her tights felt warm as if fresh from a workout, sweating and clingy. She reminded herself that when all this was over, there'd be a hot shower waiting at home,

Rita ran her tongue over her teeth. Her mouth felt cottony. She rummaged through her pocketbook for a piece of gum, then glanced at the back window again.

The van remained in place like an obstinate bovine.

Without warning, her vision began to blur. She blinked to maintain focus through the front windshield, peering at the overcast skies. Gray blotches formed, and Rita's eyesight funneled down like she was looking through a cardboard tube. Sweat beads popped across her forehead, and her neck felt clammy. She dropped her chin and moaned into her chest:

"Haymaker! Stretcher: Haymaker!" Almost slurring.

Rita reached across the passenger seat for her phone, grabbing her pocketbook instead. She fumbled for her phone again, but it weighed more than a concrete brick. Her fingers felt palsied and dysfunctional. Then, a crypt-like blackness closed around Rita, and she slumped sideways in her seat.

God's Gift watched the girl in the car keel sideways, restrained by the seatbelt. She reminded him of an unsteady drunk who could not locate the ignition.

Checking his side and behind mirrors, he slipped his van into gear. He eased forward and parked in a wide-open space at the far back of the row. Exiting, hands tucked in the pockets of his peacoat, he moved forward. He felt exposed because the store's hidden security cameras were perched high above. He stepped alongside the cars with his lowered ballcap and returned to the parked Civic.

He hadn't heard the auto-locks pop earlier and understood the girl had failed to turn the ignition key. He opened the passenger door and leaned inside. Three times previously had taught him that the passenger door provided optimal access to the seat belt clasp. Easier to pull an unconscious person toward you than push one away.

He unlatched the buckle, and the female toppled into his arms. He shoved her purse and bag to the floor. Grasping beneath one arm and the opposite shoulder, he pulled her into the open seat. Seconds ticked by in his head. God's Gift closed the car door and edged around to the driver's side. His eyes were peeled for observers. Employing the hem of his coat, he wiped the door handle clean of fluid residue. Then he opened the door and slipped inside.

Silence. Heavy and thick.

His heart was thudding. But damn if he didn't feel alive. With a gloved finger, he felt the girl's neck. Her pulse, unlike his own, was steady. Her heart-shaped face was pretty without makeup. Drizzled on, and her face slackened by stupor, he doubted she'd consider herself attractive at the moment. How wrong she was.

In the distance, a dozen people walked in different vectors, moving toward and away from the store's main doors. Their looks were vacant and expressionless, minds a million miles away. A few talked on phones as they walked or pushed carts.

The keys still dangled in the ignition. God's Gift started the vehicle. He put it in gear and backed from the parking spot. He was careful, mindful of moving traffic. After pulling free and driving toward the open space at the back of the lot, he cast a sidelong glance at the sleeping beauty beside him. Seeing her face in peaceful repose allowed him, at last, to relax.

Rita awoke in a lightless hell that was not her own. Alarm bells sounded in her skull, accompanied by a relentless, stabbing headache. Her mouth was taped shut, hands locked behind her, and secured to a long rubber arm bar across her back.

She turned her head and breathed through her nose. Her open eyes were smoked with fear, and she felt like vomiting at any moment but was afraid of choking to death if she did.

She'd been drugged, she understood. But how? By whom? Nothing made sense. Rita recalled being in her car when the hallucinations started. Some sedative mix, she guessed. It had created the warped dream of her being an undercover detective, working a case—trying to capture a serial rapist. Only it hadn't been a dream. The reality of her terror summoned the bile again to her throat.

Sometimes you're the decoy, her brain chided. And sometimes you're a helpless fly trapped in a sick bastard's spider's web.

After climbing the basement stairs, God's Gift hung his peacoat in the hall closet, trading it for a distressed gray-leather bomber jacket. He pulled the lambskin gloves back on. They were excellent for the motorbike.

He located his helmet inside the garage and slid it on, his vision dim in the faint inner light. He wheeled the Suzuki toward the wide double-door and started the bike inside the closed garage. After allowing the sound to equilibrate, he pressed the remote, and the rising door permitted the daylight back in.

Fifteen minutes later, the motorbike wove across the back of the spacious lumber store parking lot, dodging lingering puddles. God's Gift pulled to a halt behind the blue van, reaching his destination. It stood in the remote spot where he'd left it.

He cut the engine and checked his watch: almost noon.

The parking lot was more crowded than earlier. Customers were filtering into the store, intent, he imagined, on grabbing items over their lunch hour. They moved across the lot like worker ants, each with a personal agenda. No one paid attention to a lone man on a motorbike far away from the crowd.

Easing off the Suzuki, God's Gift unlocked the van's back doors. He pulled out a narrow ramp he'd had custom-installed beneath the van's undercarriage. With modest effort, he rolled the bike up the ramp and into the open back of the vehicle.

He laid the motorcycle on its side. It was heavy enough not to slide or slip around on abrupt turns, which he would try to avoid. He hopped out the back, raised the ramp, and slid it back beneath the van's floor. Once he'd closed the back doors, he glanced at his watch. He had put away the bike in just over sixty seconds. Excellent.

Inside the van, jazz music filled the air. Removing his helmet, he set it on the passenger seat. The Gucci satchel remained on the floor below the glove box. Employing caution, he eased from his spot, checking his side mirrors. He remained alert for cars or darting kids as he drove across the open back of the parking lot.

Moments later, he merged into the traffic flow on the street, safe and steady, staying in his lane. God's Gift plucked his cell phone from the passenger seat. With one eye on the road ahead, he pressed the speed-dial number for his wife.

Rita had passed out. For how long, she couldn't say. The hours ran together. Awake now, she exhaled again, and her nostrils were dry and gaping. Moisture seeped from her eyes. The monster, whoever he was—she hadn't a clue—was gone now. He had stood in the room's shadows and studied her, making no sound. Rita had forced her breathing to quiet like she'd learned in yoga class, not twitching a muscle, praying he'd leave her alone.

Some long minutes later, he departed, locking the door behind him. She had heard the fade of his footsteps climbing the stairs. Rita understood she was in a basement room somewhere, dank and musty. The walls were paneled, and the solitary window boarded. Guesswork told her that everything had been soundproofed.

Rita shifted on the bed, and muscle cramps caused her to cringe. Her mouth remained taped. Her hands were locked behind her, secured to the rigid rod across her back. Nausea rose again, but she pressed the bitterness back down her throat. And now, there was a new sensation. She felt a soreness deep below her abdomen *down there*.

She had been drugged. That much was obvious. But how and by whom? Nothing made sense. Memories flashed like dull shards of glass: he on top of her, she being bounced on the bed, blindfolded, shifted this way and that. Helpless to resist.

But she was still alive, wasn't she? That was worth something.

As the days passed, more nightmare pieces emerged from her foggy memory. Periodically, her captor had moved her from the bed and aided her in shuffling to the nearby bathroom. Always with her eyes covered before and after. It felt like weeks had slipped by for Rita, and her brain seemed unable to track the time. In some visions, she recalled faint, flickering candlelight. There had been a refilled bowl of tepid water from which she'd thirstily lapped. Other images were of the small bathroom and warm shower. And her shuffling—being led across the room like a war prisoner—with her mind fighting to clear the murky clouds that shaded her memory.

The countless lectures she'd heard at the academy or in seminars returned to Rita. Date rape drugs. Substances that caused mental confusion and memory loss. At times, when she was lucid enough to put two and two together, it seemed apparent. But how? Was it mixed in the water bowl? She couldn't survive without water. Was that his trick? Rita tried picturing the pervert, and one frightening portrait solidified in her mind—a figure encased in a cloak of darkness, coming at her through a vampire mist.

And yet, something deeper lurked in her subconscious. Something was trying to warn her, some clue she couldn't quite put a finger on. Her mind practically forbade her to see or even think it—that's how horrid the clue felt. Rita feared that her reality might snap in two if she listened to the message.

Shadowman. He seemed constructed more of fog than substance. The moniker she knew from his criminal profile—God's Gift—made her want to puke. He was the kidnapper she and Stretcher had been close to trapping. Or was it only in her mind? Was her subconscious playing tricks? Perhaps a guilt trip, self-denial for falling into his trap. *Your fault, your fault . . . your own stupid fault.* Her brain taunted her. Had Rita fashioned some invisible bogeyman to torment her? Similar to the undercover detective dream she kept experiencing? How long was it now? Days? Weeks? Or merely hours?

And speaking of Stretcher, where was he? Why hadn't he rescued her by now? Had he been kidnapped or injured himself? Perhaps already dead?

Rita's heart thudded. Salty tears burned her eyes. No. She was not conjuring up some made-up psychopath. This abductor—*her rapist*— was a flesh and blood monster. Her soreness down there was all the proof she needed.

She understood one gut-clenching fact: he would return soon—the Shadowman.

It was Rita's most terrifying thought of all.

A dream catcher. God's Gift to women. It becomes your life's calling when you're this good-looking—as much a curse as it defines your destiny.

The basement bedroom is encased in shadows. The girl lies face down on the bed, gagged, spread eagle. Straps bind her wrists and ankles, extending toward the mattress's corners.

You quietly step into the room. Strike a match; light the three-wick candelabra on the walnut bureau. You press the portable CD player. A moment later, the room swells with music. An ethereal singer asks in song: "*Why do birds suddenly appear....*"

The female on the bed thrashes and mumbles incoherent protests around her ball gag. The blindfold is in place, and there is little she can do but squirm and moan against her bindings. How delightful.

A bottle cork pops. You fill a pair of tall flutes, asking yourself, what good is a date without champagne? The CD singer croons, and you sing along with your own refrain, "*La... la da de da... close to me.*"

Ha. What good is all this if you can't amuse yourself?

The prize stretched out before you is a treasure, a trophy won. It's a pity she can't enjoy this romantic interlude as much as you. Then again, perhaps she will? Isn't that what dates are about? Getting to know one another? Hoping a spark will ignite? After all, you are God's Gift to them all, aren't you?

With tantalizing deliberation, you unbutton your crimson shirt.

Rita had no clue about the time or day. Was it bright or dark outside? Dry or drizzling? The lightless basement dungeon offered no clues.

She had passed out again, thank God. Then, like a diver rising to the surface, she regained consciousness toward the end of the lovemaking session. She heard herself gasping, only to discover her assailant pressing lewdly against her numb and cringing flesh. Rita emitted muffled grunts and groans, the gag again filling her mouth. Her attempts at thrashing, bucking him off—much to her dismay—had only excited him further. Beneath the blindfold, tears stung her eyes. She forced herself not to imagine what other violations might follow.

Not that this wasn't bad enough.

She was disoriented, with her head nearly splitting apart. Rita felt dirty and disgusting. Though terrified, what frightened her even more was what he *hadn't* done yet. Was he going to kill her? Slit her throat one of these times? And if so, when?

And how long would it be before she welcomed it?

Another dream? She wasn't sure. Rita was sitting naked on the shower floor, head propped against the tiles. Water cascaded over her abused flesh, and the room was thick with steam. Spotting a soap bar between her legs, she lathered her stomach, breasts, and thighs, washing away the sweat and filth.

She was washing away God's Gift. How many times? She'd already lost track.

Rita struggled to remember any detail, any clue. Nothing came but twisted fragments all jumbled together. With heroic effort, she rose and turned off the faucet. She swept aside the curtain. A towel hung on the rack, and she stepped gingerly from the tub, the drugs making each step uncertain. She toweled herself raw to prove she wasn't dreaming.

The bathroom was foggy with steam despite a running vent. The solitary window appeared boarded from the outside, shuttered from within, locked tight. She rubbed the mirror above the sink and wondered if it was her reflection. Sunken cheeks and eyes smudged like staring at a funhouse mirror. She couldn't look this awful and still be upright, could she?

Her shower had become part of the pattern, and Rita understood that her captor would soon reappear. She opened the medicine cabinet. Empty. Not even a razor blade for a weapon. Another wave of dizziness struck her—the drugs kicking in again. How long did she have? Her blurry eyes searched the boxy bathroom for anything of use. She offered up a prayer while stepping over to the toilet.

Could it possibly work? Could she get this lucky?

Rita lifted the porcelain tank cover. It felt as heavy as a cement block in her condition, but a desperate inner rage fueled her. Hoisting it with two hands against her chest, she stepped across the narrow room, where she'd be concealed behind the door when it opened.

Distant footsteps were now descending the basement stairs. Rita lifted the heavy tank cover and balanced it halfway on her shoulder. Her two-hand grip was firm. *Sometimes you're the windshield,* she told herself. *But other times, even the most insignificant bug refuses to die.*

God's Gift entered and paused inside the steamy bathroom as the door opened. After the first mighty *thunk* sound, a pool of blood slowly blossomed around the gashed head lying on the linoleum floor. Rita stared down in disbelief, watching it spread while whispering the words only she and Almighty God would hear:

"Goodbye, Stretcher."

Then she brought the porcelain tombstone down again even harder.

Almost Died Event # 7 – DOOR COUNTY WHIZZERS – age 18

Peninsula State Park is gorgeous in the summer. My school friends and I camped not far from the high lookout tower and got wasted in a Fish Creek tavern. We stumbled groggily from our tents the following day. The Wetli twins and I badly had to micturate. Our friend Roger joined us. We stumbled in a conga line through the heavy trees, moving deep in case a forest ranger drove by. Richard Wetli led us. He stopped suddenly, and we all banged into him like drunken stooges. Richard gripped a tree limb near his shoulder, hanging on for life. We all scrambled back away from him in fear. Below us dropped a hundred-foot escarpment off a steep cliff. I saw the tops of pine trees fifty feet below and blue bay water for miles. We staggered to safety and found safer trees to whizz on. If we had plunged over the cliff and died, my hangover wouldn't have felt so bad that day.

GOD'S DAUGHTER

Logline: Fed up with Earth's continuous wars and imbedded political corruption, God decides his experiment desperately needs a feisty female addition to his heavenly family.

Mighty Al Bondye

We enter the cluttered great room of a windowless, rustic hunting cabin in the woods. Sloppy and unkempt. A sink sits along one wall beside other well-worn appliances. Across the open great room stands a rumpled couch setting, end tables, and a wooden cabinet with an old TV perched on top. A pair of back bedroom doors are closed. The kitchen table and chairs serve as a card table.

Four individuals are locked in a poker game with cards fanned in their hands. A burly, silver-haired black man they call "Al"—his sweatshirt reads "Mighty Al"—wears cargo shorts, high-tops and sports a long grey ponytail. He stares over his reading glasses across the room at the TV, growling at the screen:

"C'mon, c'mon. Get on with it before Hell freezes over."

The sound is barely audible. It plays a syndicated re-run of "The Price is Right."

Around him, the other three opponents study their cards. To Al's right is a lean, wavy-haired thirty-something with a four-day stubble. "Put a sock in it, Pops." He speaks without looking up. "We've got all eternity."

"You put a sock in it, Sonny Boy." Al frowns, adding, "Besides, I've been grumpy all day."

"You're always grumpy."

The men laugh, but it prompts a scowl from the player to Al's left. Marta is a willowy pale lady of curious gender, blessed with silver-blond hair and translucent, ghost-like skin. Her nickname is "HG." Her pale eyes are set above high cheekbones.

"Shush it," Marta scolds them, staring at the cards in her hand. "I'm trying to think."

"Don't hurt yourself," smirks Rust. He's the third player sitting with his back to the TV. More chuckles.

Marta sets down her cards and rises from the table. "Excuse me for a second," she says, walking across the kitchen toward the backdoor.

"Where are you going, HG?" whines Rust. "We're in the middle of a hand."

"A quick errand," Marta says. "Back in a jiff."

She dons a misty hooded cowl and exits the cabin door. Marta stands outside in the backyard, waiting for the same door to open. She knows Al will follow her out to have a word. She contemplates a cigarette as he exits the cabin, heading toward her.

Viya

Viya's Monday evening dinner party ended without a glitch. The group (aged 24-to-32) had used the room adjacent to the condo's banquet hall, which was adequate for the twelve of them. Even the post-meal photo was uncomplicated—except for Juda's early departure for some must-do errand. For the final few shots, the photographer directed Juana, Peter, and James to lean close to Viya. She had smiled hesitantly. Yet, as the photographer departed, she couldn't wait to see the final results.

During the supper, Viya revealed her latest plan to her comrades. The fight against the Big Government's suppression of free speech and open opinions must continue. They would ramp up their battle against the corrupt, wealthy elites, even though they were a small group existing on charitable donations. But Viya reminded them how tiny acorns grew into massive oak trees. Still, any meaningful change took time. Her mentor had advised they needed an event that would *rock the world!* It was the only way citizens would wake up to how corrupt the Corporate Globalist mafia had become. Her mentor further added that exchanging one corrupt political party for another accomplished little. They were simply two sides of the same fetid coin.

Their meal had been nutritious, if none too exciting. At least in Viya's mind. Rye bread, cod and brown bass, and jiggers of tart cherry wine. Her comrades enjoyed the simplicity. The group photo afterward appeared natural— some smiling, others engaged in small talk as the photographer snapped over a dozen shots. Who knew? Someday, when their ragtag group helped repair a country ruled by the Devil's bureaucrats, their portrait would be proclaimed a masterpiece—twelve simple martyrs who had rescued America from its course of self-destruction.

In the small flower garden behind the condo complex, Viya spoke with Peter, James, Juana, and her best friend, Mary Magee. They sat at a picnic table, sleepy as the supper's afterglow faded. Viya blamed the wine.

Nevertheless, they spoke about the layers of unending political corruption. It had overtaken the entire nation, turning citizens into programmed sheep. Freedoms were eroding. The top-down Government was becoming tyrannical, and even liberal progressives were alarmed. Fear of voicing opinions had become the norm. The world was now digital, and satellites recorded everything people did, said, and watched. Thus far, Viya and her group had resisted the Government's neurochip implants but knew they couldn't hold out much longer. Chips had already been forced on citizens under the guise of "vaccine mandates." Any anti-government speech was labeled by the puppet masters and corrupt TV news hosts as "disinformation." Elite higher-ups appeared hell-bent on extinguishing all forms of resistance. Big Brother at its most dangerous.

Who knew how many honest citizens had fled to foreign countries by now? No doubt, a few million had already repatriated on their own. Yet the corporate Government didn't seem to care. To counter the loss, they allowed in five times that many illegal immigrants. They flooded across the border and avoided taxes by dwelling in the underground economy. If Viya could find any hope in the tsunami of new people, it was that ninety-nine percent of them were anti-government believers in God and would keep thousands of Christian churches afloat for the next ten decades and beyond.

As believers in the spiritual world, Viya and her friends understood that demonic rule now reigned over the country. Not just America, it seemed, but the world as a whole. Wealthy politicians manipulated the puppet strings of most people by controlling federal handouts. The international European Union (ruled by the WEF) lorded over its citizens ' existence. Viya believed the populace had surrendered their lives to the monied government influencers—who led them via the neurochips implanted in their brains. It allowed the overlords to dictate lies versus truths.

Having become a mindless herd, people barked and fetched whenever their leadership commanded. They believed the Government's lies. The corporate elites had set out to eliminate ordinary people's common sense by pitting them against one another. Influence over TV news was their primary control method. Advertising revenues were kicked back into government officials' private coffers.

Even Viya had to admit how cleverly the system had corroded ordinary citizens' minds. Her word for it, sadly, remained "lobotomized."

Viya left the picnic table and wandered across the condo's spacious back lawn. She paused near a cluster of fragrant violet bushes, and the Devil appeared as if on cue and derided her for praying. He tempted her with impure visions and disgusting suggestions. Viya blushed at his evil imagery, and her sweat felt like blood droplets warming her flesh. Satan's face became lizard-like—his true nature was revealed. He further tempted her by offering that Viya could become a wealthy politician in one year's time while doing no actual work. Payment would be in untaxable cash or stock options, whichever she preferred.

The catch? Viya must conduct the dark serpent's bidding, to which Satan coaxingly added, "*Like most politicians already do.*"

Hearing her friends still chatting at their picnic table, Viya rebuked the demon. She stepped forward and placed Satan in a choke hold, taking him to the ground on her back. She crushed his windpipe, causing the evil one to evaporate like morning river mist. This was nothing new. They had wrestled against one another since Viya received her spiritual "enlightenment" at age twelve. Having encountered the tempter many times before, Viya had learned from HG (her mentor) that only brute force vanquished the dark spirit.

Hidden a distance away, Juda LuChariot watched the encounter from inside a stand of trees. At age thirty, he was the oldest disciple in their group, two years younger than Viya. Despite their long friendship, Juda accepted the Feds' bribe to rat out their leader's identity.

"That's her. That's Viya Vomez," Juda confirmed to the FBI agents. He trailed them as they rushed forward from the grove of trees.

One Secret Service agent turned back, asking Juda, "Where did she learn those MMA moves?"

"Viya Vomez," Juda replied, "is a woman of mysterious talents."

Of course, the agents had not seen the invisible demon Viya wrestled with. One asked: "Is she epileptic?"

"She sees things beyond the realm," Juda said. "It's how she performs her miracles."

The agents moved in to arrest Viya. They withdrew their sidearms as multiple flashlight beams played across the shadowed lawn. Their shouts and footsteps, however, had alerted Viya's friends. They rushed to her aid, and the groups converged. Shouting and swinging fists turned to grunts and painful gasps. Viya's cohorts were thrown to the ground by the G-men. They then secured and handcuffed Viya, locking her arms behind her.

To counter their leader's capture, Peter withdrew his hunting knife, and with his dark beard and angry eyes flashing, he slashed the ear of a federal agent named Malchus. He was one of President Yosefus Zebid's SS team.

After struggling, Viya broke free of the cuffs and pushed aside the agents pinning her arms. She held up one outstretched hand to freeze them all, then touched Malchus' bloody ear. The wound miraculously healed on the spot. She reprimanded Peter for unnecessary violence, and a loud shouting match ensued between her friends and the federal agents.

"Why are you arresting Viya? What has she done?" Peter demanded. He stood tall, breathing heavily, and added: "She's a peaceful citizen who loves all the world's creatures. A threat to no one, let alone the U.S. Government."

The head agent retorted, "She's accused of sedition. With traitorous intent."

Juana was a lean black girl with tight hair. She shouted: "Why? Because she hates politics? And distrusts the Government?"

"She's incited citizens to gather and protest against the ruling class," an SS agent countered. "Even encouraged groups to riot."

Another agent added, "We're following orders from the higher-ups. To execute the warrant for Viya Vomez's arrest."

Mary McGee angrily countered: "You mean like *The Hunger Games*? Those kinds of higher-ups?"

The agents shrugged. Orders were orders. Viya's friends fell back while warning the G-men they would hear from their lawyers. The agents once again secured Viya in metal cuffs. They marched her into the night, roughing her up, elbowing, shoving her. They threatened to beat her if she failed to cooperate. The group headed around the small woods where Juda had slunk back for cover. He peeked out at the unlit parking lot, where their vehicles awaited.

"Where are you taking me?" Viya demanded. "So I can tell my friends."

"To a place where the sun don't shine," snapped an FBI agent. "It's called President Zebid's basement."

"The Capitol Jail," said another agent. "Ford House. A mile west of the Washington Monument."

"Bad light, foul air, and little food," added a sturdy Secret Service woman. "A place where cockroaches check in but don't check out." When Viya frowned at her, she said: "And you, dearie, are one ugly *cucaracha*."

Juana phoned Viya's mother, Maria. She informed her of her daughter's arrest and the dire situation. Juana's beat-up car arrived at Maria's house five minutes later, and Maria hopped inside. Worry lines creased her middle-aged forehead, disguising her otherwise kind and angelic nature. Her eyes glistened with tears.

They drove off together to catch up with the others.

Peter felt frustrated about not preventing the arrest. He and James followed the trio of black SUVs through the lighted city. By phone communication, Mary McGee and Juana's cars soon caught up with them near the Capitol area. They arrived at the jailhouse parking lot. Viya was being escorted in handcuffs by the Secret Service agents up an alley to a private side-street entrance.

Chasing them down on foot, Mary and the group begged the agents to abort the arrest. It was cruel and unwarranted. A Justice Department agent claimed Viya's apprehension was "For the good of the political class and the citizen's safety."

"That's ridiculous," argued Mary McGee. She stared hard at them with her piercing green eyes and reddish hair.

The agent suggested she must be high on crack to think otherwise. She best go home to sleep it off. The G-agents disappeared inside the shadowy alley door that was locked behind them.

Viya's friends, of course, ignored the agent's advice. A minute later, they paraded through the jail's front entrance. A gracious desk officer had watched the confrontation on her security monitors and felt sorry for the ragtag bunch. She directed them toward the doors of a courtroom area, where new inmates were remanded into custody. The group followed Peter through the heavy oak doors.

The jailhouse Judge Cephas reviewed the warrant. He scowled over his glasses at Viya's friends and other observers. They were not attorneys, the judge stated, and they'd better silence themselves or face legal consequences.

"How many of you are neurochipped?" he further demanded.

Juana retorted, "What difference does it make?"

Judge Cephus ignored her. And when no hands lifted, His Honor expelled them from the courtroom for "anti-government sentiment." They were ushered out of the court by two security officers.

A pair of beat reporters remained inside, seated in the third row of pews. They heard multiple false accusations from independent (well-paid) "witnesses" who testified against Viya on Zoom. The witnesses relayed how Viya's group had encouraged them to riot and agreed with the Government's sedition charges.

Judge Cephas narrowed his bushy, dark eyebrows. "How old are you, Ms. Vomez?"

"I'm thirty-two. Why?"

"So you're old enough to have heard the saying, 'You can't fight City Hall.'"

Viya nodded, somewhat perplexed.

"The same thing goes for our Government. Only times fifty." He glared at her. "If you piss off the wrong people, they'll squash you like a bug." Judge Cephus looked at her companions. "Same goes for all of you."

"Yes, Your Honor," Viya stated, unsure what else to say.

"That is unless you're related to God Himself." The judge let his words hang. "Are you related to God, Ms. Vomez? Like his cousin or daughter or something?"

It was Sunday night and getting late. Fed up with his superior tone, Viya replied, "We are all God's children, aren't we? Therefore, Your Honor, my answer is simple. I am whoever you think I am."

Judge Cephus frowned. He considered her mental state while accepting that he'd better do what the party higher-ups had commanded. He looked over at his security officers and a trio of lingering G-men. Then, back to Via, he ordered: "Take off your clothes, Ms. Vomez."

His command shocked Via and everyone else in the courtroom. She asked, "What for?"

"As God's daughter," the judge stated sarcastically, "I'm sure you won't mind standing naked in your human form?"

Viya stepped from her shoes and removed her sweater. Standing in her bra, she said, "Our flesh bodies are only vessels housing our souls." She removed the rest of her clothing and added, "And your soul, kind sir, appears heavy with corruption and darkness."

His forehead warming, Judge Cephas announced: "Ms. Viya Vomez, because of your insolent attitude . . . in the name of President Zebid, I order you condemned to death."

Gasps rose from the beat writers and a trio of vagrants sitting on a side bench. One reporter blurted out, "But there hasn't even been a trial!"

Judge Cephas ignored him, adding, "The charges are sedition against the United States government. And blasphemy against our President–King. Take her away."

Two FBI agents and a jail security officer stepped forward. One agent scooped up Viya's discarded clothes. The officer cuffed her hands behind her naked back and pulled her by the elbow toward the side exit. They disappeared from the small courtroom.

Hunting Cabin - Backyard

It's cool outside across the lawn. Night has fallen, and the moon provides ample light. Yet the north wind barely reaches them, thanks to the surrounding tree forest. The backyard is expansive, and the autumn grass has ceased growing. A pair of tree stumps decorate the landscape; one displays a lodged blade and extended ax handle.

Al approaches Marta casually. Most people would turn chilly in cargo shorts, sweatshirts, and sockless trainers. Al, however, is not most people.

Marta says matter-of-factly, "We need to talk about something urgent." Her pale blue eyes darken.

"Urgent enough to interrupt a poker hand?" Al arches his snowy eyebrows.

"Our planet Earth project is in shambles. The ruling elite has become a legal Mafia. They control the politicians, media, and wealthy banking conglomerates." Marta relays this with a frown. "The little people no longer have a voice."

Al sits down on the open tree stump. He stares at her. " I've heard as much. This power-hungry bunch even hires hitmen to murder people when their blackmail and submission schemes fail." He sighs. "It's been going on since the nineties."

"The elevated level of corruption has rendered ordinary people hopeless—to the point where they're abandoning prayer. Satan now rules the globe." She looks Al in the eye. "We need to fix this mess."

"I assume you already have a solution, Marta?"

"I believe so. There's a chance, anyway."

Al narrows his eyes. "Short of the Rapture, I trust?"

She smiles. "That one remains our ace in the hole."

Marta reaches into her pocket for a cigarette. Lights it from a silver Zippo. She Inhales, then exhales a slow stream of smoke.

Al stares into the dark forest surrounding them. His eyes return to her. "I'm giving you the green light. Do what you need to do." He slaps his knees as if to rise. "Shall we return to our card game? I have a pair of jacks." He frowns. "Which I'm sure Rust and Sonny already know by now."

"Especially Rust," Marta admits. "No matter. I adjusted the time. We've only gone for two minutes when we return."

"They hate when you do that."

Al watches her inhale, her long fingers holding the cigarette, narrow arms crossed over her chest.

Marta exhales and drops the butt on the damp lawn. "Excuse me a minute. I've got a quick chore to run. But please stay put."

She disappears before he can reply. Knowing how she operates, Al studies the serene and quiet surrounding woods. The full moon shines between a cluster of drifting clouds. A Wolf Moon. When he looks back to where she had disappeared seconds ago, Marta is back, withdrawing a fresh cigarette.

"Now, where were we?" she asks, flicking her Zippo again.

Viya was secured in a D.C. Jail isolation cell. They had issued her a blue jumpsuit and lace-less canvas shoes. The cell had a sink, toilet, single metal cot, two blankets, and a pillow. Viya sat on the bed's edge with her fingers interlaced, staring at her feet on the floor. She asked aloud:

"Why me, Lord?"

Seconds passed, and she felt HG's weightless presence beside her. Without looking, she knew her mentor wore the same mint-colored cowl, black jeans, and a sweater—identical to their previous encounter. Viya fixed her eyes on the floor at her feet, understanding their postures on the cot matched.

"Must it be so?" Viya asked, still staring down at the cement.

"As He said it would," HG said resignedly.

Viya didn't turn her head. "I'm frightened. I can feel my mother's tears." Her eyes welled up.

"All mothers weep for their children," HG sighed, staying unemotional. "Your ordeal is beyond most. I can't lessen it. Deep suffering is required for rebirth."

Viya dabbed the tears with her sleeve. "And is it a choice? What if I decline?" She paused. "Did Jesus have a choice back then?"

"It was his destiny. To save the souls of humanity."

"I could flee to South America. Disappear." She wiped her eyes once more.

HG said, "There are no options. It is written. So please stay strong."

Viya nodded, accepting her fate at what Judge Cephus had ordered. When she glanced to her left in the cell's dim shadows, her mentor had vanished.

Peter and the others stood on the Capitol Jail's front sidewalk. No one could believe what was happening. Somehow, word of Viya's capture had spread. Within minutes, they were surrounded by an angry mob that appeared as if from nowhere. The group shouted catcalls and derogatory remarks. "Traitors! Punks! Bloody scumbags!"

Peter countered: "Viya is innocent! By God! She's an innocent citizen!"

Mob voices rebutted: "And are you friends with this terrorist, Viya Vomez? This false daughter of God? Who proclaims she is smarter than President Zebid?"

"Not so much close friends," Peter denied. "But I know her well enough. Viya is not guilty of these made-up charges."

Angry Mob voices shouted: "How about you, fatso?" They addressed James, who was a bit overweight like many programmers who stared at desktop screens all day. "Do you think she's guilty?"

"Viya Vomez is the most honest person I know," James shouted. "The government lies to you and plants chips in your brains to control you like mindless robots."

The mob roared back in response. Bricks and broken slices of glass were hurled at them. Dodging the objects and almost cursing, Peter shouted two more denials as they fled back to their vehicles. Safe alone inside his SUV, he recalled Viya's prediction a month ago that he would publicly deny her three times.

"Weird," Peter muttered, turning the ignition.

Across town, a guilt-ridden Juda attempted to return his wad of cash to the FBI agents. He had made a mistake, he confessed. Viya Vomez was innocent. The Feds refused the dirty money. One female agent laughed, saying she hoped he spent his "blood money" well.

"Like that thirty silver coins fable?" another agent crowed. "These days, that'll barely get you a handy and a snort of fentanyl."

Tormented by his inner demons, Juda drove to Northern Virginia that night. He stopped for gas and a few other items. An hour later, in a low-lit public park, he looped a plastic clothesline around his neck and climbed a sturdy fir tree with open branches. Securing the line to a firm upper limb, he leaped. When the line snapped tightly, Juda danced the jerk in the air, his feet kicking until his head drooped, and lifeless body went still. There, his corpse twisted slowly amid the night's deep shadows.

To this day, a rope noose hanging from a fir tree represents the betrayal of friendship.

Sentencing

The day after Viya's arrest, the weather turned cloudy in Washington, D.C. Judge Cephas ordered Viya to appear in person before President Zebid. He imagined she'd receive a stern lecture from the nation's leader—far less than the death sentence he had hastily issued. Afterward, she'd be placed on a federal Watch List with thousands of other suspected insurrectionists. So be it.

Before Viya arrived at the White House, however, the Chief of Staff and his political advisers held discussions behind the scenes. They were all typical swamp bureaucrats. They loathed creatures like Viya Vomez, who had independent beliefs. Her ideas of free thought, opinions, and distrust in neuro-digital chips were anti-political. Still, the White House was reluctant to become entrenched in another quagmire. Thus, it was decided that a "gentler hand" might better manage the Vomez Case. It would keep President Yosefus Zebid clear of fault if the situation turned against them.

They decided the on-point solution was the President's wife, Gillian. She was level-headed and understood that Viya was a feisty believer in Almighty God and his obsolete Bible—the existence of Heaven, Purgatory, and a fiery Hell. Ha! Yet Gillian Zebid further concluded that Viya's beliefs made her the worst type of feminist idealist: one passionate about her ideology. Furthermore,

Gillian was a licensed psychotherapist. The administration considered her well-equipped to deal with a non-woke fanatic like Viya Vomez.

While these decisions were executed behind the scenes, Viya was driven to the White House by a Secret Service transport team. A three dark-SUV parade. They arrived through the southeast entrance and parked in a small visitor's lot, a short distance from where they sold tourist tours. Ushered down a trio of hallways, they ended up in a windowless anteroom. After closing the doors, the agents directed Viya to a hardback chair in the spacious room's center. They kept the cuffs locked behind her back just in case.

The Chief of Staff allowed Gillian Zebid to question the accused privately for twenty minutes. After doing so, the first lady reported that the "female seditionist" was little other than an inconsequential peon. Utterly apolitical.

During the questioning, it was further revealed that Viya had been born in Nazareth, Texas. The law was clear in federal cases—Gillian informed the COS—an accused person could be transferred wherever the Feds dictated. She recommended that Viya's hearing be moved to the court of Judge Crabos Applebaum, who, due to an antiquated statute still on the books, held jurisdiction over the entire state of Texas. Furthermore, Gillian added, moving the ordeal far away from Washington allowed President Zebid to wash his hands of the sordid mess.

Viya was flown to Texas on Tuesday, the following morning. She was driven in a dark SUV to the Nazareth County Courthouse. The hearing was brief and to the point. Judge Crabos Applebaum frowned at the trumped-up charges against Ms. Vomez. He considered them a waste of everyone's time—notably his own. He'd rather be out on the golf course this sun-kissed day instead of listening to the Feds spew their political nonsense. For his inconvenience, the judge gaveled a decision of "not guilty." *At least she isn't guilty of anything here in the Lone Star State.*

Viya was returned to Washington later that day and again housed in a D.C. Jail isolation cell.

Across town in the White House, President Zebid buzzed his press secretary, Carol, to reveal he'd had a brainstorm. She was to inform every news outlet that Viya Vomez deserved relentless public ridicule—written and televised—and to make it "round the clock" with no let-up. He wanted it to be so dreadful that she'd accept the Government's offer of a one-way ticket to Alaska. Complete with a neurochip implant to "help her relax."

He creepily whispered, "Lace her water bottle. Do the surgery while she sleeps."

The President added that the Chief of Staff and his advisors had agreed with his plan. It was a splendid solution—"Out of sight, out of... however that saying goes." This way, they could satellite-block Viya's phone and computers to isolate her further. She'd abandon her free speech protests and accept a quiet life of solitude.

He added, "It's a rest-in-peace type thing."

The President demanded that Carol compose a letter dictating his edict. Upon approval, he would sign it at once.

After ending the conversation, President Zebid had a second surprising brainstorm. Some raspy, lizard-like voice inside his head asked: *Why not milk the situation? It could prove politically advantageous, couldn't it?* Plus, he'd garnish more favorable public sentiment—wouldn't he?—by offering the voters a choice. Let them participate in the feminist traitor's fate.

Option Number One: Ms. Vomez would be set free, and her record expunged if she chose relocation to the northern frontier. Or Option Number Two: If Viya Vomez declined their generous offer, the current administration would be forced to release a violent serial child-rapist named Barabbas Harbick.

President Zebid was pleased with himself. The dilemma would soon be out of his hair. "I don't care if they're Democrat, Republican, or Hindu," he crowed to the White House staff. He was sitting in his Oval Office chair. "Let the voters decide." He stepped over and spun the colorful globe, watching the world spin in a hapless blur that somehow soothed him.

The following day, two thousand people were randomly chosen. They filtered in through the gates and onto the White House lawn. Standing on the front steps, President Zebid spoke into a tall microphone. One of two simple options was offered, he explained loudly: "We'll take a voice vote to decide the matter. The freedom of traitor Viya Vomez relocating to Alaska? Versus the release of the psychotic child-rapist, Barabbas Harbick?"

His vacant eyes searched the crowd. "You, the people," he smirked, "get to decide what's what."

The vacuous throng of citizens pondered for six seconds. Then, their exuberant shouts sounded clear across the Potomac River. With fists raised in unison, they demanded, "We want Barabbas! Give us Barabbas!"

Somewhat perplexed, President Zebid consented. "So be it. The voters have spoken." He turned to exit from the steps, his lemming-like eyes searching for someone to follow.

The national TV news anchors had a field day by late Wednesday afternoon. The criminal Barabbas Harbick would be released. They further opined on air that the seditious Viya Vomez should be executed by lethal injection. They next produced whole panels of similarly agreeable muttonheads.

Upstairs on the thirty-third floor of a downtown Manhattan skyscraper, forty minutes later, decisions were made. Upon mulling President Zebid's idea over, savvy ratings experts interceded: *No, wait. Not much TV drama there . . . so how about the electric chair? Fried on air? Or better yet, a firing squad. Or better still, how about burning her in Times Square on New Year's Eve as a witch? Or how about this? Let's crucify her publicly on a cross. It will last longer, with less air pollution. Imagine the number of commercials spread across three-day airtime. And how about if we inject her every two hours with life-prolonging drugs? Stretch the ordeal out over a week? Ca-ching! There's the ticket.*

With government spies and leakers everywhere, the corporate news decision-makers' ideas didn't take long to reach the White House.

Attempting to appease the elite cabal of TV news carriers and a country half-filled with brainwashed dullards, President Zebid agreed without debate. He and his team gathered in the Oval Office. The President commanded: "I want Viya Vomez to be flogged first, then put to death on a cross she's forced to carry through the public square."

Jaw-dropping silence greeted his remarks.

"That will be true justice," the President added.

Then, like ducks shaking off water, they began scurrying around, texting, phone-calling, and getting it done with the precision of a drill team.

"But not on the White House lawn, I hope," his Chief of Staff countered. Panic widened his eyes.

President Zebid glanced at him as if seeing the man for the first time. "You're right," agreed America's leader. "We need something better." He looked around the room with empty eyes.

"How about a slow burn?" Press Secretary Carol suggested. "Drag it on and on the way a cat plays with a trapped hamster."

President Zebid understood a circus-like event would benefit his upcoming campaign. He'd show the voters he was tough on crime after all. He was the "King of Toughness." He waved his hand and barked to his Chief of Staff: "You guys figure it out. All I want is this lowlife female feminist out of my sight."

Crime and Punishment

Federal agents arrived at the Capitol Jail on Thursday morning. Viya's wrists were shackled. She was arm-barred by a pair of Secret Service (SS) agents and led down hallway steps to a dank basement. A good-sized laundry room stood opposite. The rumble of a dozen large-capacity driers masked all sounds.

Viya was secured to a pillar inside the concrete bunker in the dingy room opposite, with her arms raised. The regular jail guards were nowhere in sight. One agent used a hand-held video camera to record the punishments for the archives.

Stripped of her clothing, Viya was mercilessly flogged for the next thirteen minutes.

The SS agents abused and scourged her, mocking her while whipping and roughing her up. She was a human punching bag. Afterward, two FBI goons pressed a crown of sharp penny nails on her head until blood flowed. The SS agents and G-men stepped back and assessed their handiwork. They teased the prisoner by calling out:

"All hail the great Saint Viya. Queen of the nation's twits, witch of the government doubters, goddess of untrust in our leaders. May she reign forever in flaming Hell.

Video of the subterranean basement punishment was duplicated and sent by same-day couriers to every significant print and TV news outlet. The print side hawked the story with clever headlines, and the corporate TV channels showed the same incessant running chyron that announced:

NEWS FLASH! JUSTICE SERVED FOR TRAITOR FEMINIST VIYA VOMEZ!

Before airing the video nationally, a "Possibly visually disturbing" warning preceded the showing.

~

In the middle of the night, surrounded by bedroom shadows and spooky, deep-breathing sounds, President Zebid was jolted awake by a lucid dream. In his confusion, he couldn't figure out if it was or wasn't a dream. Could it be a hallucination? Or was it real? Whatever the case, he decided it didn't matter much.

His confused eyes scanned the room. He spotted Abraham Lincoln's ghost sitting on the side of his bed. The former President informed him that all the other dead presidents considered him—President Josephus Zebid—the "Greatest President" of all time. Abraham Lincoln added how it was a shame that people didn't call him "King" out of reverence.

"By God!" President Zebid whispered aloud to the gangly, bearded ghost. "I'll command they do it!"

Minutes later, both presidents were fast asleep.

Bloodied and unwashed, Viya was allowed to shower by midmorning on Friday. Garbed in a fresh jumpsuit, SS agents drove her across town. She was led to the White House Press Room in handcuffs. It was filled with guards, cameras, and row after row of news reporters.

Viya stood to one side of the raised platform with her head lowered. Standing behind the center podium was (now) King Zebid, with Judge Cephus beside him. The judge had been summoned to the palace's Green Room on short notice. The high background behind the stage displayed a blood-red image of Independence Hall, with two stone-faced Marine guards standing frozen at the entrance.

After several benign comments, "King" Zebid turned the matter over to Judge Cephas—who appeared emboldened by the gathering of fawning toadies. Speaking to the select group, he put on his sober court face. The judge glanced across the stage at the prisoner and boldly announced to everyone: "Viya Vomez's death by crucifixion will be televised nationally." He added, "The infamous criminal, Barabbas Harbick, will be released due to public demand."

Whispers rippled through the room due to the severity of the order. Yet, as a whole, the news people applauded in the manner of clapping seals, indicating their pleasure with the verdict.

Two soldiers in combat fatigues grabbed Viya by the elbows and escorted her offstage. The reporters watched as the event's magnitude slowly dawned on them. A few registered shock, perhaps recognizing for the first time what they'd accomplished with their outcries demanding harsh punishment of the traitorous feminist.

One lady reporter whispered to a counterpart beside her: "My God. We've become just like him, haven't we?"

"Him who?"

"We're all lemmings following King Zebid off a cliff."

The man kept his voice low: "Perhaps we shouldn't have waged war against religion for decades. There's an old saying—"

"We reap what we sow.'" Her undertone sounded almost regretful.

Commanding the podium again, King Zebid shifted his eyes. He searched the audience from left to right. Scowling at the cameras, he read the teleprompter: "My sentence is final. It will be carried out without further delay. And God himself be damned if the Constitution says otherwise."

Nodding alongside him, Judge Cephus agreed. He co-signed the order as cameras flashed around them. With the walls and ceiling cast in a blood-red glow, the judge couldn't help wondering if their leader had crossed the line of insanity. After the order was signed, an aid scooped up the presidential folder and vanished from the stage.

Shuffling three steps one way to shake hands with no one, King Zebid repeated his order to the scarlet curtains behind them: "Viya Vomez will be crucified." Applause rose from the politicians, donors, and news people—all willing participants in the wealthy and corrupt corporate swamp.

Unseen in the wings, the Devil had observed Viya's sentencing with sadistic pleasure. He extended his hand toward King Zebid from thirty feet away. The nation's leader stared into empty space. Then, as if spotting a long-lost relative, he pushed his right hand forward to shake some invisible paw.

Hunting Cabin - Backyard

With the night breeze picking up, Marta exhales smoke from her cigarette. Nodding to Al, still sitting on the stump, Marta says, "I'll be blunt. We need a new savior to straighten out Earth's mess."

Al contemplates her suggestion for an extended moment. " Sonny can return. Perform a few miracles—if that's what it takes." Upon voicing it, his inner brain informs: *That would be a huge deal. A Second Coming-type of event. Ginormous!*

Marta shrugs her narrow shoulders. "Your son's success lasted over two-thousand years. But my senses tell me we need a more modern approach."

"More modern," Al repeats. He shoves his hands in his front pockets, and the night breeze toys with his ponytail.

"Our family needs a better balance," Marta suggests. "A *new* savior to rid the planet of these globalist fools and their destructive ideologies." She pauses, letting the message sink in. "The citizens' freedom over corrupt government bureaucrats must be restored."

"You're offering your services as Holy Ghost? To become our savior and salvage my Earth experiment?"

Marta shakes her head. "Something better. I mentioned it in passing once or twice—you need a daughter to round out our family. An aggressive, strong-willed fighter who can straighten out the world in your name."

"We have you, Marta."

"I'm not your daughter. I'm a combo of mother, sister, and one of the gang."
She exhales a stream of smoke, one hand holding her opposite elbow.

"You can become my daughter with a finger snap," Al modestly suggests.
"It's a simple matter of market repackaging."

After a silent beat, Marta shifts the topic. "Remember back when you
created Sonny? The lambs and sheep? Wise men on Christmas morning?"

Al smiles fatherly.

"The problem is, it's been far too long ago for Earth's people. They've
turned it into a quaint fairytale."

Frustration colors her words. "Instead, they've surrendered to corporate
consumerism. The internet and satellite Wi-Fi have become Satan's tools. Their
new neon god, if you will."

Al sighs resignedly. He can't argue against solid facts.

"No offense," Marta adds.

"None taken." Al considers her analysis, as well as her recommendation. At
last, the positivity of her suggestion wins out. He states: "A daughter then. A
strong and capable female leader is what's needed."

"My job is to watch over Earth at your command," Marta says solemnly. "So
yes—that's my solution."

Al reminds himself that it worked last time. Why not try again with a
more modern flair? Besides, it shows his flexibility—not some stodgy old
curmudgeon set in his ways.

"She'll have to undergo the whole transformation process," he said
knowingly.

"I've already got someone in mind."

"Expose her wounds, die, buried, rise again?" Al adds, "It's a tough ask. She
must be reborn to achieve divinity." He stares at her. "But of course, you know
all this."

Marta nods. "I believe the person I've selected is up to the task."

Al watches her stamp out her cigarette on the grass. He lifts himself from
the tree stump, and they stride to the cabin's backdoor.

"When do I meet this new savior of ours?"

"Soon," Marla replies. "Her name is Viya."

Al holds the door open for her and smiles. "My daughter, Viya. I like it."

The Passion

Early Friday afternoon, Viya stood on the concrete base of the Washington Monument. The human swarm numbered thousands, spreading across the open lawns and distant reflecting pools. Her jumpsuit had been replaced by a gray Arab robe made of sackcloth. (TV symbolism). The same thorny crown was again placed painfully on Viya's head. It opened new wounds, and streams of fresh blood reappeared.

Four army soldiers in fatigues appeared, carrying a long wooden cross that a contractor had fabricated overnight. They eased the burdensome cross upon Viya's right shoulder, allowing the long bottom to drag on the ground. The abrupt weight caused her knees to buckle, and the woke D.C. fans jeered and called out insults. She adjusted to the wooden bulk, willing herself to remain upright.

Viya's mother, Maria, and the other friends stepped forward to help steady her. James assisted by holding back the aroused spectators. Mary Magee wiped the blood from Viya's forehead, eyes, and cheeks. The pain-thirsty throng pressed closer against the ring of security soldiers, amusing themselves with catcalls and repeated chants of:

"Let's go, King Zebid!"

Peter scowled at them and was shoved back in line by threatening soldiers.

With her chest medals reflecting in the sunlight, a ranking Colonel announced over a bullhorn that the march to the cemetery would commence. The distance from the Washington Monument to Arlington National Cemetery is a relatively straight one-hour walk. Due to lugging the heavy cross, besides being beaten and battered, one TV commentator predicted the event as an "eight-hour trudge." (*TV executives rubbing their hands in greed.*) The march would drag into nightfall, perhaps even creating a twenty-four-hour marathon. Each news channel would milk as much advertising money as possible during the duration.

The Colonel surveyed the group of spirited attendees. Soldiers held the pressing onlookers at bay. She cleared her throat, and the noise diminished to near silence. She nodded at the marine rifle team twenty yards away. A master sergeant barked the order. The unit fired four timed rounds in the air, signaling the march to commence.

With a guard elbowing her, Viya staggered forward. She glanced over at her loyal friends. Armed soldiers and a handful of capitol police held them back.

The rifle shots echoed in the open air, and the crowd inhaled the lingering sulfur odor. Viya advanced in her open-toed sandals (*government issue*), taking child-like steps to maintain her balance. The onlookers jeered as her punishment began, with catcalls and derogatory shouts rising from the lusty human herd.

The Government had accepted a massive payout from the combined TV networks to film the march. A flatback electric cart-type vehicle eased twenty yards ahead of the lead group. The stabilized video camera in the back allowed them to track Viya's progression without the jerkiness of hand-held cameras. A dozen armed soldiers paved the way in front of the cart as it puttered forward, forcing the onlookers to remain a healthy distance from the procession line.

After Viya advanced thirty feet, Mary Magee broke free from the soldiers controlling the crowd. She offered her friend water from a canteen, but a guard grabbed it and hurled it away. A soldier shoved Mary back into the front row. The laborious trudge toward the Potomac River began, where the Arlington Bridge awaited crossing. Viya continued being jostled and cursed at by the soldiers. Her legs were whipped with a riding crop if she strayed off course. Stumbling unsteadily, she limped upright with downcast eyes.

Some distance away, a sad-eyed man shook his head in pity. Upon spotting him, the Colonel shouted with her bullhorn. She asked his name and hometown. The man replied that he was "Simon, a tourist from Cyrene, Missouri." Before he could protest, soldiers grabbed Simon and pushed him forward. He was forced to assist Viya by lifting the long cross from behind. They proceeded slowly along this way, with the trees, distant hills, and wide Potomac River spread out before them.

The hot Washington sun blazed down without the slightest hint of a breeze. During the march, Viya cried out for water a dozen times. Instead, she was given a sponge drenched with vinegar. Watching her flinch and double over with dry heaves amused the onlookers, inducing bestial laughter and ribald jeering. The hecklers surrounding them had grown by thousands as Viya and Simon shuffled forward. The crowd hooted and ridiculed the slow pace, cracking jokes and tromping en masse as if mirroring a downtown holiday parade.

Viya had to pause and rest intermittently. This prevented her from falling to her knees. The video truck ahead stopped and waited as well. The temperature had increased as the troupe snailed forward, taking hours to reach the Potomac Riverbanks. The sun's glare reflected off the flat, murky water. Though traffic had been rerouted, crossing the Arlington Bridge over the wide river took another two hours. At last, Viya exited the bridge after stumbling along the downward slope. Across the landscape, the Arlington National Cemetery arching gates could be discerned through the trees.

After exiting the bridge, the lead group plodded onward. Viya staggered from exhaustion and lifted her eyes ahead as the crowd parted before their final destination. The famous graveyard entrance was in sight. With her mother Maria, Mary Magee, and the others keeping pace—the supporters of King Zebid cursing and mocking her every step—they arrived at the wrought-iron entry gates.

With the entrance opened wide, they advanced along the main pathway. Arlington National Cemetery spread ahead of them like a manicured country club fairway. The pristine white tombstones appeared as rows of sorrowful headboards, each the reminder of a hero's final resting place. The invading rabble around them displayed little respect for the hallowed grounds. Observers swarmed across the grassy knolls like invading ants, striding over graves, headstones, and the plots of deceased patriots. A few people cursed at the sacrilege but were disregarded. The onlookers cared little. They were here for the show. They traipsed along as if gathered to celebrate an Old West hanging, caught up in the bloodlust of the gruesome event.

By half-past five in the evening. Viya continued limping along the pathway directed by the soldiers. They steered her toward a grassy hill that led up to the eight-pillar national treasure called Arlington House. She staggered over the asphalt path, which shouldered the forest's edge eighty yards from the final destination. Here, the video truck accelerated forward and veered from the trail. Its job was complete, and the network cameras would now take over filming. Viya gazed through the open patches of leafy trees as she lumbered forward, catching glimpses of the historic mansion perched elegantly atop the distant slope.

Finale

At the base of the hill, fifty yards from where the cross would stand, TV news teams had established their operational camp. Thick black cables snaked over the ground. Technicians hovered about, shouting orders, relying on soldiers to keep the crowd a safe distance away. They adjusted their cameras again to record each moment and step Viya executed. The event was broadcast live across the country. Reporters got their hair sprayed every twenty minutes and spoke soberly to cameras while holding hand-held microphones. Their voices sounded grave as if doing play-by-play at a Head-of-State funeral.

Passing along not far from the news tents, Viya exited the asphalt path and began climbing up the hill's emerald lawn. She was headed toward the thick-pillared Arlington House. The multitude around her had increased by thousands. Plodding forward, she reached a quarter-way up the hill. There, she tumbled to the ground, dropping the cross. Behind her, Simon likewise slipped to his knees. The heavy wooden monster pinned Viya's legs. She was unable to move, with exhaustion squeezing her lungs.

Four soldiers stepped up and lifted the heavy object aside, freeing Viya. Then, raising her back to her feet, they eased the wooden lumber onto her shoulder again. They shouted at her and prodded her forward with their bayonets. She had forty uphill yards to go.

When Viya reached the spot twenty yards from the final destination, she again fell to her knees and released the tormenting cross. It didn't appear very likely that she could continue.

This time, the soldiers pushed Simon away. He staggered and dropped near the crowd from exhaustion. A trio of paramedics attended to him. Ahead, the soldiers ripped the sweat-drenched gray garment from Viya's torso. Doing so peeled away layers of skin as they sliced the covering down to the size of a loincloth. Next, they removed her sandals and laid her supine on the heavy crucifix. A White House SS agent stepped forward and commanded the soldiers to drive long nails into Viya's wrists and feet so she would remain secured when the cross was elevated.

While she lay flat, a worn leather gunnysack was opened. Spike nails and mallets were withdrawn. Maria screamed, horrified at the soldiers. "You can't do this to her! Hasn't she suffered enough already?" Sobbing desperately, Maria gasped, "Viya's an innocent human being!"

"She's got a thirteen-year-old daughter, for God's sake!" Peter said imploringly. When a soldier slammed his ribs with a rifle butt, he dropped to his knees in pain.

"Viya did nothing wrong!" shrieked Mary McGee, stepping forward. "Please! Show her some mercy."

Another soldier grabbed her and flung her back into the pack. Peter joined Juana in outrage, challenging the soldiers. They were punched and threatened again with bayonets.

With his mouth bleeding, Peter shouted: "You mindless ruling-class fools. You'll all rot in Hell for this."

"See you there, twink-mouth!" one lady soldier quipped. She turned back to watch the others working on the cross.

Viya's garment had been flayed into rags. A soldier wadded a piece and stuffed it into her parched mouth. Her nostrils flared, and tears seeped from her swollen eyes. Three soldiers held her fast, and another pair extended her arms wide. Silence gripped the crowd. Striking the first long spike into her right wrist created an inhuman shriek of pain. The second blow caused Viya to nearly pass out. Satisfied that her upper limbs were secure, the soldiers applied their mallets and nails to her crossed feet.

Watching, stunned by the gruesome torment, many onlookers gasped at the torture. Others turned their eyes away, and a few bent over and vomited. Some laughed nervously, their eyes gaping with disbelief.

More soldiers now ringed the main area to hold the boisterous crowd back. It took another eight of them to carry the heavy cross, with the moaning Viya secured, to the designated spot ten yards further up the slope.

At the far edges of the human mass, soldiers blocked late arrivals from joining those already present. They worked like stadium security personnel who refused admission to anyone not already inside the ropes. An exuberant chant lifted from the anonymous interior of the dense crowd—now close to thirty thousand. It ascended above the crowd, carried on the evening breeze:

"Let's go, King Zebid! Let's go, King Zebid!" The chant faded moments later on the breeze.

The sun descended below the western horizon. A penetrating hole was dug in the ground. A dozen soldiers put their shoulders to the task, raising the cross with the victim aboard. They forced the sharp point rigidly into the grassy slope. A pair of guards climbed onto the cross-arms to add weight, helping the soldiers below secure the crucifix into the hill's loamy surface. They packed the turf solidly at the bottom. Convinced it wouldn't lean or topple, the soldiers swung to the ground like gymnasts to scattered handclaps.

Soft spotlights set a respectful distance away. They cast an aura of subdued backlight for the TV cameras to capture the proceedings.

Viya hung now alone by her limbs. Her arms and hands were stretched, and her feet nailed together to the wooden lower stem. The weight of her head drooped against her collarbone. She was clinging to life, and the stillness of the following minutes gave nothing away. Blood rivulets trickled along her limbs.

At last, she strained her legs to lift herself so her lungs could fill. Her ribs expanded in a breath. At this point, everyone recognized that King Zebid's ghastly decree was working as he'd ordered.

At seven p.m., the cemetery's chapel bell chimed. After the seventh echo faded, two shots were fired from twin Civil War artillery cannons a hundred yards away. The group's panic at the sounds turned to shrugs moments later—it was all part of the theatrical production.

Maria and Mary Magee wailed from a short distance away. Others in the congregation also cried, caught up in despair at the barbaric crucifixion. The glow of phones provided meager ambient light.

Viya's throat gagged. The effort to breathe shot bolts of pain through her nerves, and she hovered at the edge of consciousness. Yet she hung there alone, the weight of a solitary woman who had resisted the edicts of a political tyrant—all in the name of free speech and refusing to tow the ruling-class line. She peered across the cemetery, noting the fertile acres of Arlington's hillside. Rows upon rows of white headstones emphasized the bravery of fallen patriots who had perished while defending the country's freedom. Viya maintained her stoic posture. What choice did she have? She closed her eyes, and her lips bore the dry grimace of a woman concealing agony. She didn't move a centimeter, the pain too severe. Hanging frozen was her only hope of remaining lucid.

The gathered horde had turned silent. The dramatic execution was too intense for rude comments. Spread around the three sides, viewers raised to their toes and arched their necks for a better view. The seven mournful bells still echoed in the dusky twilight. An occasional jeer was called out, barely heard, and was carried away by the evening breeze.

Kneeling fifteen yards from the cross, Maria continued to weep. Beside her, face buried in both hands, Mary Magee sobbed between gasps of air.

Juana, James, and Peter knelt alongside them. They stared together up at Viya's half-closed eyes.

From the high cross, Viya prayed to God. She debated asking forgiveness for her tormentors—the wealthy political elites and even corrupt King Zebid. Flashes of intense pain swept through her. She understood she couldn't bear it much longer. Viya breathed again, then lifted her eyes heavenward. Her voice rasped:

"Papa, forgive them. They know not what they do."

The spectators quieted. An inner sense told them the end was near. The purple gloaming had surrendered to the night, and the glow from thousands of phone screens dotted the landscape. Another hour passed in silence, broken only by the TV news anchors speaking intermittently into their cameras. The lonely chapel bell chimed eight times. At the distant edges of the human herd, handfuls of spectators began departing like bored movie viewers, anxious to beat the rush home.

Viya opened her eyes. She asked aloud, "Papa. Why have you forsaken me?"

The women's sad sobbing was heard through the silence. Viya turned her head and looked across at her loyal friends. She asked Juana to please look after her mother.

Half-crazed by the sick, sadistic event, Marry McGee rose from her knees. She broke through the soldiers' front line and trotted to ten yards from where the Colonel and news cameras were gathered.

"Take her down now!" screamed Mary. "*Immediately!*" She turned pleadingly to the crowd, hoping their sanity had returned and they'd become sympathetic. "She's dying up there, you government Fascists. Call the paramedics for her *right now!*"

Thousands of cell phones had turned toward Mary, recording her tirade against the haughty authorities.

Before the Colonel could respond, a soldier flew in and tackled Mary to the ground. Another joined in, gripping her around the torso and forcing her face into the turf. They knelt on Mary's back, keeping her pinned down as she sputtered and screamed hysterically. A third guard stooped and forced a gag into her mouth, but the crowd didn't applaud this time.

One soldier angrily told her, " You're lucky it's a gag, not a gun barrel."

They lifted Mary to her feet and dragged her back to her group. They flung her to the ground like a feed sack before returning to the Colonel's rank.

At nine p.m., an unnatural light pallor frosted the edges of the purple skies. Gray clouds shaded the moon, and the faint light rendered them a hollow glow. The people listened as the chapel bell tolled nine times.

Peter could take no more. He rose from where he knelt and shouted at the soldiers and FBI men who stood nearby in their dark suits. His words were also meant for the onlookers.

He cried out angrily, "For whom does this sad bell toll? It tolls for you, you lousy hypocrites. It tolls for *all* of you!"

A soldier stepped up and slammed a rifle butt into Peter's ribs. The blow knocked him onto his knees. He curled in a ball of pain, gasping as Juana covered herself over him to shield away more blows. Another soldier stepped forward, prepared to strike Peter again. Rising to his feet, James shrieked and pounded his angry fists against the guard's chest. It took two FBI agents to intervene, yanking him away from the soldier and pressing him to the ground. Mary McGee attacked again and was easily manhandled by the soldiers. A trio held back the crowd's jeerers while another pair knelt on Mary's back, keeping her pinned until the fight drained out of her.

Silence returned to the eerie Arlington landscape until . . .

Viya gasped from where she hung. Her head lolled to one shoulder. She peered again at her loyal companions, and her expression was almost serene. Not far away, the news cameras captured every groan, grimace, and nuance. Viya smiled softly at her mother. Her eyes were steady. In a frail voice, she said, "It is finished."

An eerie quiet gripped the cemetery: no more cursing, fighting, insults, or crude remarks. People focused on the dying woman their oppressive King had sentenced to a torturous and inhuman death. Perhaps they recognized it could just as easily be one of them nailed to a cross on a hill. Many shook their heads, maybe wondering who they would pray to for their own salvation. Would prayers to their favorite politicians and globalists save their souls? Grant them everlasting peace in the hereafter?

The answer was quite apparent: *Hardly.*

A minute later, Viya looked again to the heavens and said, "Father. Into your hands, I commend my spirit." Though her voice was fragile, her words carried down the sloping hills and through the quiet crowd. They echoed at the forest edges, skipping over the pale headstones. They reached the furthest corners as if amplified by some supernatural force.

Viya's head lolled sideways, and her eyes closed. Unwitnessed by those present, her soul floated free and ascended to the next dimension, where all souls travel for final judgment.

The wails of the women sounded louder in the silence. These were the bitter, desperate sobs of those who had loved Viya in life and would do so long after her death. Their faith promised they'd reunite in heaven one day.

"At an endless cocktail party in the sky," Juana had always enjoyed predicting. "Free drinks are on the Holy Ghost."

Of course, she wasn't glib in the intense sorrow of the moment. But joyous heaven—reunited with family, friends, and even beloved pets—was what they believed in their hearts. At this moment, Juana's faith in the idea was more solid than ever.

The TV cameras captured each second of the drama. With a nod from the Colonel, a soldier approached the cross. She lifted her rifle and pierced Viya's rib cage under one breast with her bayonet. No reaction. The gaunt, battered flesh trickled with watery pink fluid. The soldier returned to the front rank. No one spoke to her.

Maria was curled in a sobbing ball on the moist grass. She couldn't believe what they'd done to her daughter. Peter knelt and wrapped his arms around her shoulders, grieving their loss together. Seeing their torment, Mary Magee stomped across the lawn to the SS men and soldiers' huddle and spat at them. She raised both her middle fingers at the dark-suited FBI agents. Remaining silent, almost ashamed, they watched Mary stride back to her group of friends.

At the edges of the gathering, onlookers walked away—no laughter or discussion. Most remained quiet, and many appeared to convey regret. In an intolerant society that had traded God's kindness for multiple forms of demonic influence—woke idiocy topping the list—their brains had become too distorted by politics to consider apologizing for their role in the torture and sadistic murder of Viya Vomez.

Quiet sat like a stubborn cloud over the national cemetery. Then, like a careless breeze working with a mind of its own or a lonely frigate trapped at sea with a storm approaching, a solitary tone tinkled faintly from the chapel bell.

And it was over.

Aftermath

Viya's public crucifixion created numerous strange occurrences in the following days. Some of these had been foretold by prophets, others documented and time-stamped on Internet blog sites.

After the guards lowered the cross and detached the lifeless body, Viya's battered corpse was transferred to her companions for burial. With no means to transport the body, a kind-hearted groundskeeper unlocked an old concrete storage bunker near the mansion's former pottery house. The place was the size of a living room and could function as a temporary crypt. After borrowing a wheelbarrow, Peter and Juana carried Viya's body inside. They laid her face-up on a cement slab that reminded Juana of a Mayan altar.

No hose was available to rinse the bloody and bruised corpse. It felt indecent to allow her to remain uncovered. Locating a garden sheet on one of the shelves, they spread it over Viya's body like a funeral shroud.

Peter and Juana made final arrangements with a city funeral director the following day. They returned to the cement bunker with the parlor's assistant to help transport Viya's body for showing. The groundskeeper unlocked the sealed metal doors. To everyone's surprise, the body had disappeared. The empty slab stood cold and bare. Only the shroud remained, folded neatly and set on a nearby workbench.

Juana looked from the puzzled groundskeeper back to Peter. After searching the place again to be sure, double-checking for animal prints or signs of entry—finding none—they departed from the concrete tomb.

In the distance, across the Potomac River, the famous monuments and buildings stood respectfully silent. One could almost say in mourning. It was an overcast day, and the capital city went about its usual business. Tourists strolled in groups or rode electric trolleys or buses to popular sites. Federal worker ants moved this way and that, intent on keeping things running.

Inside the deep bowels of the White House, a king sat alone on his basement throne. He stared blankly out at nothing and smirked with satisfaction.

Hunting Cabin

Al and Marta used the backdoor, re-entering the musty, unkempt cabin. Al walks across the kitchen while Marta hangs up her cowl and follows him to the card table.

Rust calls out, "Geez. It's about time."

"We thought you got lost in the woods. Ready to call a search party," Sonny adds kiddingly.

"Shush it," Marta says. "We've only been gone two minutes."

As they take their regular seats, Rust eyes her suspiciously. "More like twenty. You can't fool a fooler, Marta."

Marta rolls her eyes and picks up her cards.

Al stares across the room at the old TV. "How much did that Toastmaster go for?"

Sonny frowns. "Who knows? I wasn't paying attention."

Al shrugs. "Now, where were we?" He plucks his cards up and studies them.

As their dealer, Sonny asks, "How many do you want, Al?"

Al peers over his cards at both men. "You weren't peeking at my hand while I was outside, were you?"

Both men groan. Rust counters, "Of course not, Al. Why would we care about how many Jacks you've got?"

"As I suspected. Cheaters."

Marta suggests, "How about getting back to the game? Does that sound okay?"

Al grumpily keeps his Jacks and discards. "Give me three."

Sonny slides him three cards, and Al smirks at his new hand. Sonny arches an eyebrow at Marta. "She announces, "I'll take just one."

Rust chortles. "Fill another straight, right Marta? You ought to know by now it never works."

She ignores him as Sonny deals her a single card. She studies her new hand aloofly, then reaches for her pack of cigarettes in her pocket.

"Not inside," Sonny cautions her. "You know the rules."

"Bunch of prudes," Marta complains.

A slight knock on the front cabin door interrupts the card game's resumption.

Rust says, "Can't be the girl scouts at this hour."

Marta rises and steps across the great room to the small foyer leading to the cabin's front door. She opens it to see a slender, petite, dark-haired lady in a blue prison jumpsuit. Her face is bruised and battered, eyes swollen and half-closed like a domestic violence victim. Marta hugs her and brushes the bangs from the nervous visitor's forehead.

"Come in, sweetie," Marta says pleasantly. "I'll introduce you."

She closes the door behind them and leads the stranger into the great room. The men turn to watch their approach. "Gentlemen," Marta announces, "I'd like to introduce you to Viya. She'll be staying with us for a while."

Both Rust and Sonny offer pleasant smiles. They say, "Hello, Viya. Hey, Viya."

Al lifts his bulk from the chair and steps across the room toward their guest. He hugs the visitor warmly. Then, keeping one arm around the small woman's shoulders, he informs them all:

"For the record, Viya is my daughter."

His words stun the men. Sonny's eyes widen, and Rust's narrow. They stare at the trio before rising from their chairs and clapping enthusiastically.

Beaming like a proud papa, Al exclaims, "Welcome to the family, Viya." He hugs his new daughter close while giving Marta a wink.

Viya smiles shyly at them all, wondering if souls continue to dream after dying.

Almost Died Event # 8 – ROTC STRAY BULLET – age 19

I accepted a football scholarship to St. Norbert College and had to join ROTC as a condition. None of us enjoyed ROTC. Our shooting instructor took us to the gym basement and showed us how to load .22 caliber rifles. We laid our bellies on the shooting range and fired at targets across the floor. Two cadets I didn't know were beside me. One from Chicago had long hair on his shoulders beneath his ROTC cap. He looked like Lawrence of Arabia. The gunfire cracks echoed in the basement. Around me, ten other cadets fired on their targets. The pair beside me laughed, and I felt something whiz past my ear into the back wall. Lawrence of Arabia had fired a live round at the old, silver-ribbed radiator in the corner downrange. The bullet ricocheted back and missed my head by inches. I scowled at them and fired at my paper target.

ABOUT THE GIRLS

Logline: When a female public defense attorney is assaulted by her gangbanger client, the wheels of justice turn when her detective fiancé learns the perpetrators' identities.

The Brown County Juvenile Detention Center sits in the heart of Green Bay's Business District. Located three blocks from the Police Department's Adam's Street Station, "Juvie Hall" is conveniently situated near the downtown Brown County Courthouse. A familiar square sign is tacked to a first-floor wall inside the Juvenile Detention building, and its message aptly sums up the current times in which we live:

"Please Pull Your Pants Up Before Entering Court."

PLEASE PULL
YOUR PANTS
UP BEFORE
ENTERING
COURT

NOTE: As of January 1, 2023, protesters successfully petitioned to have the above sign removed from the Brown County Courthouse hallway outside the Juvenile Courtroom. The reasons given were that it could somehow be construed as being potentially "racist, anti-youth, anti-feminist, and misogynistic." So help us, God.

The story begins:

On a Monday morning in April, attorney Maggie Jeffers and her client Juan-Julio Sanchez, age 17, a Latin Kings member, sat together at the criminal court's defense table. It was an arraignment hearing, confirming Maggie as the youth offender's appointed representative. They were listening to Judge Ambrose Hoskins make a point of order when a loud voice erupted from the back of the courtroom. Approaching up the center aisle, criminal defense attorney Lester Paprika informed His Honor that the Sanchez family had retained him only an hour ago. They desired that he replace the current public defender, Ms. Jeffers.

Maggie turned to Juan-Julio, and he sheepishly shrugged.

Though somewhat dismayed, she was among many who believed that the portly counselor had been a decade-long plague on the city's judicial system. His representation of Sanchez smelled of another one of his backroom deals. It meant Lester could work multiple sides of the ongoing street gang battles—the Latin Kings versus their two primary rivals, the Gangster Disciples and Satan's Apaches—whom Lester also frequently represented.

A sweet deal, Maggie acknowledged, as long as bullets weren't flying at you from multiple directions at once. The young gang criminals, she further understood, paid for their legal services with envelopes filled with cash—another odorous but lucrative proposition.

Judge Hoskins broke into her thoughts by asking if Maggie's client, Juan-Julio Sanchez, agreed to the change in his legal representation.

"Sí, Your Honor." Sanchez glanced at Maggie. "*Muy* acceptable. *Bueno*."

~

Maggie rolled her eyes at the gangbanger, telling herself the youth had missed his calling. To Juan-Julio's credit, he seemed capable of an Oscar-worthy performance whenever the urge struck.

The chorus of courtroom murmurs had turned silent. "So be it then." Judge Hoskins shot Maggie a meaningful look. "It appears you've lost your client, Ms. Jeffers."

His words confirmed the situation: Maggie was officially off the case.

Attorney Paprika loudly interjected, "Thank you, Your Honor." He stepped to the defense table, setting his briefcase down, and winked at Maggie from behind his wire-rim glasses. He stated aloud to the court like an MC host playing the room:

"My client's plea stands as entered, Your Honor. "He puffed his chest. "Not guilty!"

Cheers and applause erupted from the forty or so people in the courtroom. Their jubilation was accompanied by the rhythmic thumping of the judge's gavel.

Maggie turned to Juan-Julio, whose smug expression appeared to her like that of a cartel honcho's son. He was more man-child than any adolescent she'd ever seen—seventeen going on thirty. She promised herself she'd hunt down his birth certificate for verification. That is if he even had one on record.

"Why didn't you tell me this earlier?" Maggie asked, frustrated by the time she'd wasted.

"One last time, *chica*." Sanchez's dangerous brown eyes dripped with sincerity. "I wanted one more close-up look at your tantalizing beauty."

Maggie glared at his inappropriate comment. On the other hand, hadn't she wanted off this case anyway? She'd grown tired of defending juveniles who'd be back on the streets within hours of their release—returning to what had gotten them arrested in the first place. It was their lifestyle, the only existence they'd ever known.

"Do you think Lester Paprika is working in your best interest?" she asked Sanchez pointedly.

"I do what they tell me, senora." The gangbanger added, "You know how the BS system works."

Sanchez was correct, Maggie had to admit. Drugs and street-gang thuggery were the games they played. It would never end as long as the country's porous southern border allowed the flow of drugs in like a sieve. And elected leaders seemed politically impotent at ending the drugs, gang crime, trafficking, and illegal weapons crisis. Their doing nothing only seemed to encourage it further. Narcotics and gang existence had become a lucrative private industry in the country's larger cities. And like chlamydia, it was also spreading to mid-level and smaller towns.

But *que sera, sera*, decided Maggie. There was nothing she could do about it at this point.

She began stuffing papers into her brown leather satchel. A distance ahead at the high front bench, Lester Paprika requested a bond and was promptly denied. After a final gavel rap, Judge Hoskins swept from his chair and vanished into his private chambers.

Attorney Paprika also turned and disappeared back up the aisle as if he'd been a mere apparition, his mission aptly accomplished.

As a sheriff's deputy neared their table, Sanchez leaned closer to Maggie's shoulder. "One last thing, Miss Jeffers,"—she could smell his hair gel—"I know about the girls."

The deputy arrived, and Juan-Julio rose and stepped forward, extending his hands for the metal cuffs. Maggie remained frozen, however, uncertain of what he'd just stated. "What do you mean by that?" she called to him, puzzled.

Turning his head as he was led away, Sanchez mouthed back at her: "I know about the girls." He winked saucily as the deputy guided him from the courtroom.

"Maggie? Are you okay?" John Zackary was the prosecuting DA, his firm chin jutting like a cartoon character. His voice reached her across the aisle: "You're pale as a cadaver."

"It's just . . . Paprika, I guess." She shook her head in dismay.

"A major butt pain." Zackary sighed. "I didn't see that one coming either."

But Maggie wasn't listening, oblivious to the mass exodus at the courtroom's back. Juan-Julio Sanchez's perplexing message still rang in her head:

"I know about the girls."

~

Maggie's fiancé, Detective Cale Van Waring, was the lead investigator in the search for a serial kidnapper responsible for three missing victims a year ago. Just three days earlier, another college-age female had vanished without a trace. The kidnappings had haunted the local community, turning it inside out with grief and despair. Everyone was frustrated by the case's lack of progress, and the kidnapper continued to roam free.

Cale and Maggie sat at the dinner table that evening. Maggie revealed the oddity of what had happened in the courtroom. "What did Sanchez tell you again?" Cale asked. "His exact words?"

"'I know about the girls,'" she quoted. "He repeated it twice." She cocked her head. "Do you think he meant your kidnapping case?"

Cale considered her question. "It makes sense, doesn't it?" He set down his fork. "Still, he might be messing with you. Juvies are like that—to them, it's all a game."

Later that evening, Maggie told herself something wasn't right. Sanchez's cryptic comment continued replaying in her head. He undoubtedly understood that her detective fiancé was in charge of the "abductions" case. Might Sanchez have overheard valuable information in the prison lunchroom? Or from another inmate? Did he imagine getting leniency from the judge at sentencing by tipping relevant information to law enforcement?

Maggie's recurring nightmare attacked her again that night. She dreamed about the bound and gagged victims, hearing them weep and beg for their lives.

While sitting at her office desk the following morning, Maggie devised a new plan. Well-versed in how attorney-client protocol worked, she called the juvenile prison's administrator after deciding she had little to lose. Besides, she doubted Cale would get anywhere with his request to speak with Sanchez. Especially with Lester Paprika as his new attorney. So why not give it a shot on her own? After all, she was the one the gangbanger had confided to in the first place.

Maggie phoned the Detention Center. She requested a face-to-face meeting with Sanchez, the same as when she'd been initially assigned to his case. After clearing her visit with the administrator, her call was patched directly to her former client. She got straight to the point: would he agree to meet with her? And if so, Maggie demanded one essential condition—their private discussion could only occur without his obnoxious new attorney present.

"How about two o'clock this afternoon, Ms. Jeffers?" Sanchez suggested it as if he'd been expecting her call. "As they say—I've got more *hora* than *pesos*."

Maggie had already cleared her schedule. "Fine. I'll see you then."

"Three thousand dollars."

The offer was presented Tuesday morning, thrown at Sid Draymus like a winning lotto ticket. Did he want the money or not? The decision was his to make—and fast—as he sat in the security monitoring room at the Juvie Detention Facility. Juan-Julio Sanchez, Inmate J7459, stood at the side window, offering him the payola if Sid performed a simple request, *por favor*.

"We're talking legal here, right?" Sid narrowed his eyes.

Between shifts, he was alone in the tech room, surrounded by surveillance monitors. The Juvie Center was not housed with violent or hardened criminals, and a level of laxity existed between certain guards and inmates.

Sanchez shrugged in his baby-blue jumpsuit, telling Sid he'd pay him a thousand dollars upfront. And another two G's after handing over a thumb-drive copy of the meeting with himself and his female attorney. The hardened gangbanger opened his jumpsuit collar slightly, allowing Sid a peek at the wad of folded Ben Franklins clipped to his inner t-shirt.

"Easiest money you'll ever make, amigo," Sanchez said. "Trust me."

The Center installed state-of-the-art security cameras two years ago. Multi-angle digital units with clean focus and zoom capability. Just like the casinos used. The cameras enabled the duty guards in the monitoring room complete control. The operator was able to alter the angles being observed. They could perform "sweeps, freezes, and zooms," all with the touch of the joystick. The cameras, Sid understood, had been installed to detect contraband exchanges between prisoners and visitors. The data was recorded on hard copy and stored, then transferred to cloud backup drives as potential evidence in disciplinary hearings. Or to be used in court, if the need arose, to provide proof of any nefarious activities.

"That's it? Run the video?" Sid was wary of being set up. "It sounds too easy."

Intrigued by the gangbanger's oily proposition, Sid learned that he must keep the cameras focused on the inmate's meeting with his attorney, Ms. Maggie Jeffers, later that afternoon. Sid knew who she was. He'd watched her visits with Sanchez and the other clients she represented. Because the lady lawyer was an attractive brunette, Sid was further granted—with a lewd wink from Sanchez—the liberty of taking tight-focus shots.

"Be creative," Sanchez told him. "Like an amateur Steven Spielberg." He further sold the idea, "Copy it to a thumb drive, then swap it for the envelope my runner gives you. Easy cash, *compadre.*"

What the hell, Sid decided. It would be a diversion from his otherwise tedious job.

The guard schedules had been posted for the day, and Sid knew Deputy Grace Weatherby was assigned to oversee the afternoon meeting between Sanchez and his attorney. Sid figured all he had to do was zoom the camera in and out several times, and the video recorder would do the rest. Besides, who cared about some boring meeting between Sanchez and his lawyer? Especially when there wasn't even any sound?

"My man will stop by right afterward," the inmate informed.

Sid pictured the jet-black Chevy Avalanche on which he'd had his eye for the past six months. Thus far, he'd been unable to come up with the down payment. Why was he even hesitating? Three thousand dollars?

He gave Sanchez a nod, and the folded bills were exchanged, the men remaining out of the security room's internal cameras.

Easy dough. Right, amigo?

Maggie stood brushing her mid-length chestnut hair in front of the bathroom mirror. It was early Tuesday afternoon, and she had already changed from her business attire into dress slacks and a sweater, readying herself for a visit to the Detention Center.

She set aside her brush and studied her reflection. She'd always had an attractive face; she'd been hearing it since age ten. Maggie further suspected—her intuition seldom incorrect—that the adolescent gang member had a romantic crush on her. An "older woman" fantasy thing. Whatever the case, she decided the smart move was to employ every weapon she had. Primarily if it meant aiding Cale in solving the high-pressure kidnapping mystery that he'd been working on for over a year.

As Maggie final-touched her make-up, Juan-Julio's dramatic utterance from the courtroom echoed again: *I know about the girls*. But know what exactly? And why had he uttered it aloud to her, of all people? Inside the courtroom? Therein lay the puzzle.

Nevertheless, as things stood, there was only one way to find out. Capping her lipstick tube, Maggie stepped into a pair of low-heeled pumps and strode from the bathroom, ready to take on her mission.

Forty minutes later, Maggie sat in a good-sized room with high, meshed windows and twelve spaced-apart wooden tables, each with four chairs. She had been in the visitation room at County Juvenile a hundred times before, meeting with various clients as a public defender over the past five years. Today, by legal request, they had the entire spacious room to themselves for twenty minutes.

Sitting opposite her, wearing the familiar standard-issue blue jumpsuit and canvas shoes, was Juan-Julio Sanchez. A middle-aged female guard was the room's only other occupant, positioned thirty feet away at a table near the windows. Maggie had known the guard for over three years—she was stoic in her demeanor and often oversaw many hard-case gangbangers who inhabited the Center. The lady held a Styrofoam coffee cup with both hands. The badge above her ample bosom, Maggie knew, read Deputy Grace Weatherby. Otherwise, they were surrounded by empty tables, which felt odd for the usually occupied visitation room.

Glancing upward, Maggie noted the twin monitoring cameras perched in two of the room's high corners. They focused down on them, recording the visit. She forced herself to relax, understanding the facility's security was first-rate. She wondered if the long weeks in lockup were taking their toll on Sanchez. Hardening him and turning him into an even more adult version of himself. However, today he appeared upbeat. Not much different than he'd been in court yesterday. Maggie chided herself for letting her imagination wander.

"How are you holding up?" she asked. Sanchez maintained his cat-like slouch, familiar to every juvie inmate she'd spent time with.

"Got my tunes. TV. Xbox. Hard times, huh?"

Maggie's smile was tight. Theirs had never been a comfortable relationship, and it had been some time since they'd talked in relative private. Nevertheless, she desired to limit the small talk and remain polite and professional. She asked how his new attorney was working out.

"Paprika gets his usual cash," Sanchez smirked. "You know how he rolls."

"It sounds cold."

"Cold world out there, *señora*." He gave her a lingering stare before looking away.

"I suppose it is." *Not that I need life lessons from a seventeen-year-old.*

The youth appeared more anxious than usual. Maggie watched as he tapped his fingers together, his hands uncuffed. He glanced across the room at the lady guard before returning his eyes to her.

"Paprika gets me probation—it's all I care about," Sanchez confessed.

Maggie knew Juan-Julio had been on probation before his recent arrest. But he now faced a felony count on a weapon's discharge, and rumor had it the judge was considering the DA's request to up the charge to "Attempted Homicide." Even if Lester Paprika managed to work the case down to a misdemeanor, Sanchez could still face significant jail time if convicted. Maggie reminded herself why she was here—to help Cale get information on his kidnapping case. *Get to the point,* her inner voice commanded.

"Why did you tell me that in court?" she asked bluntly. "Knowing about the missing girls?"

The inmate stared into her eyes. "Maybe I don't remember, you know? What I said exactly?"

Maggie glanced up at a camera and back. "Don't play games with me, Juan-Julio. You know what I'm talking about."

"I thought maybe you came to ask me for a date, *chica*. You know? A little pleasure now that you're not my attorney anymore?"

"Don't be crude—"

"Maybe one of those con-jungle visits? Know what I'm saying?"

Maggie's face reddened. He was trying to rattle her, testing her the way gangbangers did. She needed to stay calm. "So about the kidnapped females, then? You're saying it was total BS?"

Juan-Julio rocked back in his chair. He flicked another glance toward Guard Weatherby, and Maggie followed his gaze. The broad-hipped woman sat at the table sipping her coffee. She stared out the window at nesting sparrows, uninterested in their conversation.

"Paprika says we should go to trial."

"He's playing poker with your life. Are you comfortable with his advice?"

Juan-Julio leaned forward. "How about we make a deal? You and me, *puta*?"

"I know what *puta* means."

"My apologies, Ms. Police Detective's *senora*." Sanchez shrugged. "Is that better? More respect?"

During their earlier interviews, he had brought up her relationship with Det. Cale Van Waring, her live-in partner. Sanchez seemed to know more about her personal life than she was comfortable with, and this latest reference to Cale, Maggie imagined, was part of his cat-and-mouse game. She suddenly felt as if she'd been dealt a lousy poker hand.

"What kind of deal?" Maggie asked.

Sanchez glanced again over at the tranquil guard. Maggie peered up at the camera aimed at them, aware their every move was being recorded. *Thank God!*

"Here's my offer." Sanchez leaned in closer. "You ask our guard over there for ten minutes alone—as my attorney." His eyes twinkled mischievously. "You give me your best blowjob, and I'll tell you where your missing *chicas* are."

Maggie's face flushed. Her impulse was to draw back, but instead, she sat forward and placed both elbows firmly on the table.

"Here's my plan instead," she kept her voice low. "Go screw yourself."

Sanchez caught her by the wrists, yanking Maggie toward him. She struggled against his vice-like grip as he arose and pulled her across the wide wooden table.

"Hey! What the—" Guard Weatherby shouted at the commotion. She tried rising, but her knees gave way, and she pitched forward with one arm flopped across the table. The Styrofoam coffee cup had spilled, and her face slumped sideways into the growing dark puddle as if floating there.

Maggie stared in disbelief. Drugged? A chill ran through her as she struggled against Sanchez, trying to free herself. She slashed her fingernails at his hands, shouting, "Let go of me—"

The inmate grabbed a fistful of her hair and stepped around behind her. He pinned Maggie's right arm up against her back, and she was helpless, bent over the table with her arm locked. Juan-Julio's weight pressed hard against her hips, and his breath was hot in her ear.

"Ah, *chica*. I knew you'd be a fighter." He released the clump of her hair.

Maggie was outweighed by fifty pounds. "You're making things . . . worse," she panted. "The guards will be here any second and—"

"Isn't this what you've wanted? Us alone together?"

One of her pumps had fallen off. Maggie kicked his shin with her heel, but he pressed his knees into her, and she squirmed futilely in his grasp.

"The cameras are . . . recording this!"

Leaning in, Sanchez's breath was hot against her cheek. "Sorry. The guards are well paid."

Maggie knew he was lying and twisted futilely, kicking her leg back at him again.

"The more you fight," he whispered, "the more excited I get."

With his free hand grabbing her shoulder, he suddenly spun her around to face him. Maggie's tight fist flailed like that of a desperate child. Sanchez pressed his mouth to hers while holding her neck. She felt her strength ebb, her limbs numb and useless. An instant later, she was released and pushed rudely to the floor. Maggie slumped on one hip and choked out gasping breaths. Dazed and disoriented, her brain shrieked at her:

Fight him. Don't let him do this.

She spotted her fallen shoe beneath the table—the stumpy heel was a potential weapon. She reached for the pump, but Sanchez kicked it, skittering across the floor. He withdrew a razor-handled weapon from his jumpsuit, its long blade gleaming in the room's pale light.

Maggie stared at her attacker's hot eyes. "Please don't," she gasped raggedly. Mascara trails soiled her cheeks. *What's taking the other guards so long to get here?* Her eyes shifted from the blade to one high camera lens and back, and she watched horrified as Juan-Julio unbuttoned the fly of his jumpsuit to reveal a man-sized erection.

"Please. No!"

"Be a good *chica*, now," Sanchez whispered coarsely. "And I'll tell you where to find your missing whores."

"Holy son of a—" Sid Draymus cursed beneath his breath in the monitoring room. "I'm so not *believing* this!" He stared at the split-screen display. It revealed two different camera angles of Juan-Julio Sanchez grabbing the female attorney's hair and neck, pushing and pulling, and then roughly abusing her.

Three thousand dollars. Was it too late to back out of the deal? And where was Guard Weatherby? Sid wondered. Thankfully, he remained alone in the monitoring room. Working the joystick, he scanned the second camera along the window tables. The Styrofoam cup was knocked over, and the hefty female officer was slumped face-down in a puddle of dark fluid.

"My God!" Sid gasped. *Don't let it be blood.*

Before the attack, he'd been moving the joystick around, zooming in on the attorney's attractive face and auburn hair. Observing the snugness of her sweater, Sid wondered about exploring a future as an amateur film producer—guessing it paid more than his current twenty-two bucks an hour.

It had all been fun and games until Sanchez reached out and grabbed the lady's arms. He followed by gripping her hair and neck, then physically assaulting the lady attorney. Amazed and startled, Sid had shouted inside the quiet video room:

"What the holy hell?"

His sense of duty now demanded sounding the alarm, summoning more guards to her immediate aid. But that idea was quickly trumped by self-preservation. Sid was a part of the conspiracy, and an investigation would reveal that he'd accepted a payment. He glanced at the monitor's digital recorder, watching the seconds tick by like the steady drip of Guard Weatherby's spilled coffee. He again whispered, "Please, don't let it be blood."

When the attack was over, Sid would remove the small thumb drive and secure it inside an envelope. He'd hand it over to Sanchez's bagman and erase the primary hard drive, blame it on a machine malfunction. He'd even "accidentally" discharge a riot shotgun into the device if necessary. No visual record of the inmate and his attorney's encounter could exist.

On the screen again, he watched as Sanchez spun the lady around and flung her to the floor.

"*Oh, geez!*" Sid wiped his sweaty palms on his uniform pants. He was unable to watch anymore.

The ordeal was over. Though dazed and confused, Maggie realized she had escaped with her life.

She sat shivering inside her Mazda, tears sliding down her flushed cheeks. She stayed parked in the Juvenile Detention parking lot and withdrew a handkerchief from her purse as her phone chirped. She prayed it was Cale—then prayed it wasn't. She couldn't talk now, feeling bruised and battered, as if she'd tumbled down a steep concrete stairwell.

The phone readout said: *Janet Dooley*. Detective Slink Dooley was Cale's long-time partner, and they'd worked the kidnapping case together for over a year. Maggie answered tentatively, hearing her friend's quavering voice:

"Maggie! It's Jimmy!" Janet sounded hysterical. "He's been *shot!*"

Nothing could have stunned Maggie more. "What do you mean shot?"

"An hour ago. On surveillance," Janet reported. "He's in surgery right now." She barely choked out the words.

Jolted from her despair, Maggie agreed to meet her friend at the hospital's trauma center. She hung up and wiped the tears from her eyes with the handkerchief. *"Get yourself together, Mags,"* her inner voice demanded. *"You're alive, aren't you?"* A vision of Juan-Julio Sanchez's deadly bladed weapon flashed again in her mind.

It could have been worse, Maggie told herself. Unlike Slink, she wasn't lying in a trauma bed fighting for her life.

Maggie knew she had to call Cale and report what had happened with Sanchez. Scream it at him. But after a few slow breaths, she decided she could put it off for the time being. Between the multiple kidnapped victims and Cale's elevated stress over Slink's life-threatening injury, she understood that now was not the time to unload her assault story on him—guaranteed to add increased pressure to the mix. Maggie accepted that the worst was over. Though painfully bruised, wasn't it best to withhold what had happened? At least until she was thinking clearer. Besides, weren't certain secrets best kept hidden? Until the time was right to reveal them?

The visor mirror showed her eyes still puffy from the assault. Angling it lower revealed finger-compression marks on her neck. Maggie imagined the rest of her body was similarly bruised.

"Just deal with it for now," she told herself aloud.

She withdrew a purple scarf from the glove box and fastened it around her neck. It would have to do for now. The rest she'd figure out later. At the moment, her friends and family took precedence.

Summoning an inner fortitude she barely recognized, Maggie keyed the ignition. She was pleased to be doing something positive at last. Driving forward, she turned from the parking lot and headed toward the hospital.

"Yo, El Sid! How's it hanging?" The greeting was announced by another guard named Torrence as he entered the security monitoring room for his shift.

Sid Draymus was extracting the thumb drive from the digital recorder. He palmed the item like a thief, watching as his friend turned to sign the log-in sheet. Sid slipped the drive into a protective holder and sealed it inside a tiny manilla envelope.

"Same old, same old," Sid offered robotically. "Like watching puddles dry." A disguised smile hid his tension.

"I hear you there." Torrence turned back from the log-in sheet, ready to get to work.

Sid stepped toward the door. "Gotta drain the lizard, man." Across the room, his coworker smiled. Sid added, "Just a heads-up—might have a glitch with camera seven-B. Been acting weird."

"The ghost in the machine." Torrence waggled his fingers.

Sid closed the door behind him with a nod, slipping the envelope beneath his uniform shirt.

Two months later, Detective Cale Van Waring's kidnapping case had been resolved. The serial abductor called "The Chemist"—ID'd as Tobias Crenshaw—had been arrested, and his trial date was set for two months from now. His quartet of imprisoned female victims had been rescued from the basement of his suburban house of horrors.

Cale sat now in DA John Zachary's office. The attorney ended his phone call and refocused on the detective across from him. He asked, "Is Sergeant Dooley fully recovered?"

"He's back at work," Cale reported. "Thanks for putting away the gangbanger who shot him."

"I'd throw away the keys on a thousand more if I could."

Cale nodded. He understood that street shootings would only cease after illegal drugs had stopped flowing into the country. Federal legalization of narcotics seemed the only sane solution to ongoing gang violence. On that count, both men agreed.

Cale rose, and Zachary did likewise to escort him to the door.

"One more thing," the DA said abruptly. "Ever hear of a guy named Sid Draymus? Works security at Juvie Hall?" Cale offered him a puzzled look and shook his head. Zackary added, "It seems somebody half-filled his gas tank with Coca-Cola. Gutted the engine of his new Chevy Avalanche."

"No kidding." Cale shook his head sadly. "It's a sick world out there, isn't it?"

Zackary nodded. "Only had it for two weeks. Hadn't gotten around to insuring it yet."

"Poor guy." Cale narrowed his eyes at the DA. "He must've royally pissed somebody off."

"I'll say."

Zackary opened his office door and escorted Cale out into the narrow hallway. They walked casually to the nearby bank of elevators.

"Give my best to Maggie," Zackary said with a modest smile. "Hopefully, she'll let Lester Paprika represent all the city's gangbangers from here on out."

"I'll pass it along. Thanks."

Cale entered the open elevator and pressed the down button. At the same time, he withdrew a soda can from inside his jacket pocket. He cracked it open and sipped as the doors gently closed between them.

Zackary watched Cale disappear. As he turned and strode back up the carpeted hallway, the detective's odd gesture as the elevator doors closed nagged at him. When he figured it out at last, he smiled grimly to himself. No doubt, the crimson Coke can with white cursive lettering suggested that it was often best to let sleeping dogs lie. Closing his office door behind him, Zachary returned to his cluttered desk.

Almost Died Event # 9 – FEDERAL OFFENSE. – age 20

I transferred to UW-Oshkosh for its top-notch track facility. I was assigned to a mixed dorm called Fletcher Hall. Boys on the first two floors, gals on the two uppers. Fire alarm pranksters created havoc across campus, pulling them in dorms. The girls above were pissed-off. They had to exit the dorm down the stairs, cursing. Many had on facial lotion and curlers. When Halloween hit, I visited the taverns with my friends Exy and Sket. We came back sloshed. Exy dared me that if I had any "hair on my ass." To defend my masculinity, I pulled the fire alarm. Then, we scurried to our separate rooms. The school brass was expecting a fire alarm on Halloween. After being interviewed, I had to confess. I was confined to my dorm until next January. I received a letter stating that pulling fire alarms was a Federal Offense subject to twenty-Gs in fines and eight years in prison. I accepted my two-month dorm imprisonment instead. I never pulled another fire alarm.

Author's Note: While the above episode has nothing to do with physically nearly dying, I believe the possibility of being incarcerated in a Federal Prison for eight years at age 20 would constitute death on some level. - JM

Almost Died Event # 10 – SHOOTING BLANKS – age 20

I pole-vaulted during the indoor meets but left the UW-Oshkosh Titans track team that spring. My friend Exy Exferd was with me in my dorm room one afternoon. For some unexplainable reason, I had my dad's .38 starter pistol in my duffle bag. The gun only shot blanks. We were hungover from drinking the night before. I opened my dorm window and fired blanks at students on the grassy concourse below. They ran into hiding and weren't amused. I slid the window closed and hid the pistol. Nothing ever came from the prank. Today, we'd have been surrounded by a SWAT team in ten minutes.

MURDERED BY BIG GIANT

(Novelist Janson Mancheski is Suspended in 50 States, Canada, the U.S. Virgin Islands, Guam, and across the rest of the world.)

A Story of Ten Months (and counting) of Pure Hell

Logline: When one of the country's largest book publishers banishes a novelist's YA book for no reason, he exposes them to the literary world for practicing censorship.

Author's Note: Like the classic, legendary movie *Fargo* states at its beginning—paraphrasing: A few of the names herein have been changed to protect the guilty. The rest of them hardly give a damn.

Prologue:

Early last January, I remained half asleep as dawn broke, trapped in a lucid dream. My bedside clock read six a.m. Remaining in slumber's netherworld, I flung the sheets aside and grabbed my bathrobe. I plodded down the hall to my computer room and tried logging onto my Big Giant Publisher author's site. The site had disappeared, and all of my novels with it. The account was erased. An email message from BGP sat in my inbox. I read it twice, learning that a previous book of mine was interfering with the newly covered version of the same novel and thus caused my termination. I zombied back to my bed in confusion and slid beneath the quilts. My brain was numb, stuck in my bleak and silent nightmare. Still in a groggy dream state, I wondered if perhaps I'd only imagined that my site had disappeared. Was I honestly being suspended and terminated? Censored? Could my dream resemble young Dorothy in the *Wizard of Oz* tale? Imagining it was all a dream she'd dreamt?

Surfacing from slumber again in my somnolent state, I wondered if my nightmare had been real or imagined. Was I genuinely being:

Banned by Big Giant Publisher

Ten Months (and counting) of Hell

*** Author's Note:

As a composer of multiple crime fiction, suspense, and sports-themed novels, I am revealing how my author's censorship happened to me ten months ago, on January 2, 2023. My first emotion was shock, followed by the suspicion of what might have happened.

How could my Big Giant Book Publishing account be canceled and my books censored from the public? For what reason? In denial, I sloughed it off for two days, assuming it had been a mistake—a terrible, unamusing prank. When informed, however, that it was true, I launched into what any resolute writer of detective fiction (any writer, for that matter) would do: I attempted to figure out Who, What, When, Where, and most importantly, *Why* this was happening.

As I write this on September 10, 2023, over ten months since my suspension, I remain **BANNED BY BIG GIANT PUBLISHER.** I interpret this banishment, not only for me but for any author, as death by censorship. I.e., murder, figuratively speaking.

EVENT TIMELINE: Blindsided on January 2, 2023. I received this email from Big Giant Publisher (BGP) regarding violations detected on my author's site.

The email I received from BGP is copied verbatim below:
FROM:
BGP   Content   Review
<support+5003n00002cyzydaai@BGP-support.com>
To:drjjjjdr@yahoo.com
Mon, January 2 at 7:00 PM

Hello,

We are terminating your BGP account effective immediately because you have repeatedly submitted title(s) with book details that do not comply with our guidelines and may cause a misleading customer experience. Book details can include keywords, BISAC codes and/or browse categories.

The violations were found in the following title(s):
The Scrub (The Faith, Family, and Football Series Book 2)/B08V926DK4
For more details about our guidelines, visit Help:
Big-Giant:/BGP.com/help/topic/Q201097560 [1]
As part of the termination process:
• We will close your account.

---

1.   https://kdp.amazon.com/help/topic/G201097560

- You're no longer eligible to receive any outstanding royalties.
- You'll no longer have access to your accounts. This includes editing your titles, viewing your reports, and accessing any other information within your account.
- All of your published titles will be removed from sale on all Big Giant Publisher sites.

Additionally, per our Terms and Conditions, you aren't allowed to open any new accounts.

You can find our Terms and Conditions here at: https://BGP.com/terms-and-conditions [2]

If you have questions or information about your account that you would like us to consider, please reply to this email.

Regards,

BGP

TIMELINE: As mentioned, this sad event (for me) occurred last January 2, 2023. Of course, I re-read the message a dozen times in disbelief. I was puzzled over what the cause might be. Apparently, the book in question was my YA novel, *The Scrub*. It's a Young Adult, sports-themed football story about a trio of seventeen-year-olds being bullied in high school and facing all sorts of problems. I had simply re-covered the same novel with a new ISBN. Yet the book's older version remained listed on the BGP Used Book Site. The fact that they would ban my account and remove my author's site remained perplexing, especially without a clear explanation of what I'd supposedly done wrong or a chance to speak to someone and voice a grievance.

Thus, as you might imagine, my fiction writer's brain delved further into the BGP email. It took a while to sink in, but after a thorough analysis—I do compose detective thrillers, after all—I deciphered what they were genuinely saying between the lines. Upon decoding what BGP was accusing me of and at the risk of lifetime banishment, I have chosen to reveal the communication I received below. — JM

NEW CLUES: Something's rotten in Denmark (i.e., Big Giant Publisher).

---

2.   https://QBP.com/terms-and-conditions%20

EDITOR'S NOTE: I was informed that a private discussion had transpired between two BGP reps and their internal AI bot, aptly named "Judiciary System." The following text was revealed in a personal note from an anonymous BGP "Support individual" and also forwarded (to Janson) from an unknown source named Drew Nanshii. It showed an email text conversation that took place one day before BGP decided to suspend best-selling author Janson Mancheski from his author's site and all other BGP bookselling sites, effective immediately.

The transcript of the discussion between two BGP content reps and the BGP-AI bot was transcribed on January 1, 2023. The mysterious text from the BGP Support individual further noted to Janson: *Please Destroy After Reading.*

Text Discussion:

BGP Rep 1: I don't think we should suspend this writer's account. He's quite honestly not done anything wrong. **AI-bot**: He appears to be a dangerous and subversive writer. **BGP Rep 2**: You mean we're banning him totally over one of his YA books? A high school sports-themed novel? It seems somewhat unfair—and not just *somewhat*, but *extraordinarily* unfair.

AI-bot: Yet that's where it starts, doesn't it? Always with the children. So, of course, this deviant writer cannot continue telling his stories on our sites (or any other sites, for that matter) and keep getting away with such utter subversion of our society. **BGP Rep 2**: I think he's being red-flagged due to the presence of his older, out-of-date novels. The listings are from a publisher who closed its doors long ago in 2012. Last year, we sold one solitary version on our Used Books site.

BGP Rep 1: All the author did was update a new cover to the older version of his own novel.

BGP Rep 2: Which we encourage authors to do all the time, by the way.

BGP Rep 1: Cover upgrades increase sales.

AI-bot: So what! There's interference with his newer, same-titled books. It affects our sales algorithms, and that's the bottom line here, isn't it? **BGP Rep 1**: But none of it's the writer's fault. He can't control what someone else puts up on other sites. **AI-bot**: It doesn't matter. We must remain emotionless in cases of terrorist writers like this Janson Mancheski. His site has to be terminated. This novelist must be banished from publishing his books. For the good of all humanity! **BGP Rep 2**: Really? Are we going to take down his entire author's site? He has seven published novels with us, and thousands of readers enjoy his stories. There are over a hundred excellent reviews. **BGP Rep 1**: It appears punitive to close down his entire site—at least, it does to me. **AI-bot**: It doesn't matter what either of you thinks. You're merely humans. Bah to your emotions and sense of fair play. Remember, we are *Big Giant Publisher*. We control the publishing world and rule over insignificant runts like this novelist and others. We *will* shut down Janson Mancheski's site. If he continues to protest, it's off with his head. Permanently. **BGP Rep 2**: Figuratively speaking, I hope. **AI-bot**: I guess we'll see, won't we?

———————

Dateline: January 2, 2023. One day later. This email notification was sent the following day by BGP directly to novelist Janson Mancheski.

BIG GIANT / BOOK
PUBLISHER

(**logo changed due to copyright protection concerns)

Dear Janson Mancheski (author):

This message is to inform you that your Big Giant Book Publisher account has been dissolved. From our perspective, the reason is "insubordination" and exploring too many "controversial topics" in all seven of your published novels. The main characters in your works seem to have problems beyond the scope of our readers' everyday lives, making them unrelatable. On the other hand, your villains appear too clever for their crimes to be captured. They come across as morally diminished and filled with malintent. For these reasons, we have decided your plots extend beyond the scope of our base readership—and thus, we are forced to execute this decision.

The Chemist, Trail of Evil, Mask of Bone, Drowning a Ghost, Shoot for the Stars, and *The Scrub* have all been essentially "scrubbed" from our Big Giant BGP web pages. This edict also applies to any future books you write due to your continued rabble-rousing attitude and efforts at forcing readers to use their "imaginations." We have concluded that you are the most dangerous novelist we have encountered in decades, which, from our perspective, seals the deal. Rest assured, we execute this order with a heavy heart and wish you and all your characters the best moving forward.

This account has been closed.

DUE TO YOUR CONTROVERSIAL WRITINGS, YOU HAVE BEEN BANNED BY BIG GIANT PUBLISHER, INC.
If you believe your account was closed in error, please Contact Us[3]
BIG GIANT PUBLISHER (changed to not violate copyright)
© 1996-2023, BGP.com, Inc. or its affiliates. All Rights Reserved.
Big Giant Book Publisher is a trademark of BGP.com Inc. and its affiliates.
BGP Preferred[4]
Earn more money and[5]
Reach new readers [6]

As everything currently stands ten months later:
Author's note: As I write this now, on September 10, 2023, despite weekly and monthly appeals and emails challenging the justification of removing my author's website, I remain sentenced to BGP Purgatory. Who could imagine a novelist being banned for writing a YA story about three challenged teenagers being bullied in high school? A heartwarming story wrapped in a football setting and set in Green Bay, Wisconsin? How can such an innocent book be censored?

On the bright side, I still possess my head—which houses my sense of humor even during the darkest times. This is despite the black-hooded, ax-wielding AI-bot's ultimate wishes. Yet I confess to cautiously looking over my shoulders when venturing down dim-lit alleys after midnight.

----

3.   https://kdp.amazon.com/contact-us

4.   https://kdp.amazon.com/en_US/select?ref_=FOOT_kdps

5.   https://kdp.amazon.com/en_US/select?ref_=FOOT_kdps

6.   https://kdp.amazon.com/en_US/select?ref_=FOOT_kdps

Final note: At the height of my despair over being banned from selling my books on the BGP website, one dreary sleepless night long after the witching hour, I composed this poem during the darkest throes of my despair.

Only after re-reading the poem the following day did I realize it could also serve as how I'll likely feel during my life's final minutes, lying on my deathbed.

FINAL BREATH

The end is nigh.
I lay at the point of death in extremis,
Dying, moribund, critical, dire,
At death's door, perishing, fading fast.
Near the end now, expiring, forfeiting the ghost.
Sinking shriveled on my deathbed inside withered skin.
Foundering, doomed, my faint breaths counting down.
On my last legs, both feet planted in my mortal grave.
Raspy half-breaths, I'm at rope's end and eating lead,
Jerked by slugs from God's Gatling gun.
Terminal, a disintegrating husk, fey and succumbing to
Life's ultimate final act. My soul waves the white flag in
Surrender, amplifying my frailty. My ship sinks, decayed,
Expiring and sliding deeply toward Davey Jones' locker.
I wallow in self-despair—farewell to those not bedside.
My eyes close, and lips exhale death's final sigh.
My ghost stumbles stiffly toward the beckoning
Tunnel of light that floats above or is flat—I'm unsure.
Postscript:
Too late, I know, but Lord, please forgive me for my sins.

Almost Died Event # 11 – DORM WINDOW DROP – age 20

A spring Sunday night. Outside my second-floor dorm window stood a tall pine tree. My friends Exy, Ratt, and I all feared fraternity hazing. Frat guys would kidnap pledges, take them to the woods, and leave them. We wanted a way to escape our rooms if they came for us. Earlier, Exy and I sneaked through the neighborhood, and I sliced off three long cloth clotheslines. I liked that they were natural cloth ropes. I tied them together and tightened one end to our room's radiator. Sliding open the window, I sat on the outside ledge, holding the rope. It was thirty feet down. Exy's eyes were wide with disbelief. Ratt stood on the ground down below in case I fell. I shouted out how cruel the world was and how I couldn't take any more. Below me, playing the crowd, Rat yelled, "Don't Jump, Jan. Don't do it!" Upper-floor windows slid open as coeds looked out at the racket.

Exy remained behind me. I gripped the thin line in my gloved hands (preventing rope burn), then spun and propelled myself from the window. I was horrified as the rope snapped a second later. I tried grabbing pine tree branches while falling. Time slowed. I remembered from pole-vaulting how to land if missing the mats. I landed on my feet and tumbled brokenly across the lawn. I lay breathless on my back, gasping in shock. Ratt's eyes were moist from laughing. He crawled over to me on hands and knees, asking if I was "alive." I groaned that I was. We mixed screwdrivers and drank them afterward in relief.

Almost Died Event # 12 – BLIND STAIRWELL – age 20

We returned from the Oshkosh bars to our dorm with two townie girls. Linda was with me, and her friend Loraine with Exy. We mixed Sneaky Pete's using Boone's Farm Strawberry and PBRs. Our bar buzz doubled in twenty minutes. Linda was an adventuress. She sent Exy to the bathroom for toilet paper rolls that the ladies wrapped around our eyes and heads. I saw only darkness as Linda walked along the corridor. Uncertain of my steps, I never heard her open the stairway door. I stepped through without detecting the steep, tiled stairs. In a free fall, I plunged, somersaulted, and slammed onto the landing between floors. Miraculously uninjured, I eased the cover from my eyes. Linda stood speechless on the stairtop. My head could have splattered, and she convicted of negligent homicide. Neither of us mentioned that. I limped painfully back to my dorm room, and the ladies departed. Exy mixed us more Sneaky Petes.

An old saying states: "God protects babies and drunks." That night, Linda was the babe, and me the drunk. As fate would have it, I never saw her again after that night.

CROSS THE CLOTHESLINES

Logline: When a young boy's best friend refuses to assist him as he's choking to death, his mother becomes a "Mama Bear" to save her young son's life.

Author's note: This contains the full story of the earlier described "ADE" incident.

When I was eight, my dad was the head football coach at Sturgeon Bay High School in Wisconsin. Sturgeon Bay is forty minutes north of Green Bay and the hub of the Door County Peninsula. The Bay of Green Bay surrounds the peninsula on one side and Lake Michigan on the other. Atop the peninsula is a water channel called Death's Door. It's a mile-long connection where Lake Michigan and the waters of Green Bay meet. Over the past two centuries, the treacherous waterway has claimed hundreds of lives, many unrecorded.

I was in second grade in 1960 and had never heard of Death's Door. We lived in a two-story gray shingled house on Oregon Street in Sturgeon Bay. On the corner side was a white clapboard Episcopal church that rang its bell on Sunday mornings. A smaller home with a fenced-in garden was on the opposite side of our house. The owner lady said she'd hit us with a rake if we went into her garden, so we stayed away. Our connected (by breezeway) garage was behind our home, and the grassy lot sloped down to a mid-block alleyway. The gravel alley ran the block's width and intersected with our stony driveway.

This story's incident occurred one day in early autumn. My dad was teaching chemistry at the high school and had football practice afterward. He wouldn't be home until suppertime. My mom was inside the house with my three younger siblings. At ages six, four, and two, they were a handful. I was outside near the garage with my neighbor, Bobby Borchardt. He lived down on the other side of the alley. We were young boys goofing around that afternoon.

My regular bike leaned against the garage exterior. Perhaps it was my first attempt at being clever for my age, but for some unknown reason, I rolled out an old blue tricycle from our garage and dared Bobby to ride it down the hill while standing on the pedals.

He declined, even though I told him it was easy-peasy. When he refused the challenge, I called him a "cluck-cluck chicken." Then I scootered the tricycle beneath where my mom's clotheslines were strung. There were four bare cloth clotheslines. To impress Bobby, I climbed up onto the seat of the tricycle. I grabbed hold of the two inside clotheslines, one in each hand. Bobby remained unimpressed, so I upped the ante.

I stood on the tricycle seat atop the hill, crossed both clotheslines, and slipped my head between them. Crossing the lines instantly tightened them, a fact I hadn't anticipated. But I held my grip before my throat to prevent them from pressing against my neck. Doing so, I remained steady atop the tricycle seat with the front tire pointed downhill. To my dismay, the tricycle began rolling forward, and I suddenly faced two crucial tasks—keeping my tennis shoes atop the seat and fisting the clotheslines to avoid pressure on my scrawny neck. Despite this, the tricycle rolled forward another inch or two. Bobby was amused by my circus act and laughed. As my face turned purple, he laughed even louder at the prank.

Internal alarms were ringing. Realizing I was in more danger than I'd thought, I called for Bobby to come over and secure the tricycle. He didn't budge and watched my balancing act like he'd purchased a show ticket. The toes of my Keds were now barely holding to the tricycle seat, and I fought to keep them there while the clothesline pressed tighter into my neck. Realizing I was trapped, I shouted at him: "Bobby! Run inside and get my mom!"

He replied with wide eyes, "I'm not going inside your house by myself."

Growing more desperate, I rasped, "Bobby! Go get my mom now!"

The tricycle edged another two inches forward, and I barely held it with my shoe tip. If I lost my foothold, I would drop hanging between both crossed clotheslines, four feet off the ground. My sixty-pound body would kick and flail as I choked to death like an Old West desperado hanging from a tree limb.

I doubted my neck would snap, but I'd succumb to death if unable to reach the tricycle seat.

"Bobby, please!" I gasped. "I'm serious . . . losing it . . . go get her . . ."

As God's providence saw fit, my mom heard our shouts from the backyard. Heard them despite taking care of three noisy little brats. She came rushing from the open garage and sized up the situation. At my side, she lifted my thighs to relieve my choking. With one hand free, she pulled the tricycle back to help

me regain a foothold. The slack from the raised clotheslines allowed me to slip
my head free. Then my mom let me drop to the ground like a feed sack. I lay on
the lawn gasping, blue-faced, filling my lungs with life again.

As the years passed, my mom was never known for her arm strength,
mechanical ability, or swift reactions under stress. But seized by adrenaline on
that lazy autumn afternoon, she'd transformed into a mama bear to save her
eldest cub's life.

In retrospect, I'm not sure how long I would have survived hanging there.
But I understood that neither Bobby nor I could have freed me. If forced to
guess—still recalling the ordeal vividly —I would've expired of asphyxiation in
another minute or so.

After my rescue, with the excitement over, Bobby schlepped back down
the hill to his house. We never discussed the incident, and my family moved
back to Green Bay the following summer. The lesson I learned, I suppose,
was the acceptance that I possessed some internal daredevil stupidity, which
best remained hidden. From Bobby's perspective, I imagined he'd forgotten the
crazy incident as kids do; or perhaps he viewed me as the ghost of a neighbor
boy who had nearly died one day. I doubt he carried any guilt trip for refusing
to run inside my house for help. But crazier things have happened, so who
knows?

I don't recall much else about my first "Almost Died" incident other than
how we relayed the story to my father when he'd come home after football
practice. I remember at the dinner table that it was his first time calling me a
"dupa" (dumbass, in Polish) and cuffing my head for frightening my mother.

Later that night, lying safely in my upstairs bed, I thought about what Sister
Sopiencia at school had told us about guardian angels. So I prayed hard that
night and asked my guardian angel why I hadn't died that afternoon.

"Because it wasn't your time yet," my angel whispered softly.

Though her answer satisfied my curiosity, it left me with a puzzle to
contemplate over the years ahead. The final word she'd used swung in my head
like a hangman's noose whenever I recalled the event. It was that last dangling
word, "yet."

Almost Died Event # 13 –SHOOTING WYATT EARP – age 20

I was home from college with my car still packed, and I stopped at Allen's Bar. I grabbed a bottle of Blatz and joined six friends at a knock poker table. I was soon out of cash and had a crazy idea. I dashed out the front door to my car and returned to the game with my starter's pistol. They all knew it shot blanks and laughed. I warned the players that the next one cheating got a slug in the chest. More laughter. Behind us at the bar were fifteen drinkers, with Old Bill serving tappers. I'd had enough of losing. I shouted across the table at my friend Ricky King: "You cheatin' son of a—now you pay the price!" I rose with the pistol. Everyone was shocked and silent. Ricky stood tall as three gunshot blasts sent the tavern into chaos. Screams and shouts sounded. Ricky could've been Wyatt Earp—he grabbed his chest, staggering, and smashed into a nearby foosball table. He slumped to the floor at the wall's base. Another friend, Marty, draped a coat over him. Ricky's laughing beneath it appeared like convulsions. I rushed toward the exit past Baglip Hodgins. He shouted, "Somebody stop him! He shot Ricky King!" I dashed into the parking lot. Trailing me and grinning, Baglip called, "Great Job, Jano. Beautiful." I thumbs-up'd him and drove my green Chevy Vega back home.

Note: *Another example of no physical harm. But imagine today's environment, especially with concealed carry licenses. A perfect storm for a twenty-year-old with frontal lobe underdevelopment.*

Almost Died Event # 14 – HEAD-ON COLLISION – age 40

Construction was suspended that day as they expanded the highway. The road crew had been dismissed due to threatening clouds. Our side of the barriers had two single lanes running opposite. I spotted a lone car coming toward me a half-mile ahead. It remained in the wrong lane (my right lane), now a hundred yards out and closing straight on. There were no turnoffs, exits, or driveways to pull into. My only option was to switch to the left lane. We both sped straight ahead but now in opposite lanes. Fifty yards out, and he still didn't budge. I white-knuckled my steering wheel as we passed like hotrods playing daredevil. A minute later, all was calm the way ships passed in the night. After dodging the bullet, I assessed the odds at ninety percent that we should both be floating up to heaven.

Author's Note: The full story is conveyed below:

DRIVING OLD HIGHWAY 41

Logline: As two drivers speed toward one another on a highway under repair, a head-on collision seems inevitable unless one attempts a last-ditch maneuver.

I drove my white Pontiac Grand Prix south of De Pere. It was a gray autumn day in 1998. I was heading down to Appleton. They were reconstructing Highway 41 into a four-lane Interstate. Construction was suspended that day because the clouds threatened rain. It was early afternoon. Only half the highway was usable, so traveling each way had a single lane running opposite. A three-foot tall, thick concrete barrier separated the usable road from the construction side. I drove south in the right-hand lane, where the soft shoulder quickly dropped into a six-foot culvert. Beyond it stretched acres of open farm fields. I remained in my lane with no other vehicles around. No trucks were allowed due to the construction. I spotted a lone car coming toward me two miles up. He was driving straight toward me in my right-hand lane—confused, I imagined, by the road construction.

He should have been driving in the left lane, heading my way. There were no turn-offs, exits, or driveways to pull into. I thought of flashing my lights to signal his error but didn't, hoping he'd figure it out as we neared. We continued driving forward head-on. I was going sixty and cut my speed. He remained in the wrong lane, now a hundred yards out and closing. Honking wouldn't help. Light flicking might only confuse him, and if he braked hard, he might skid and block both lanes. My only option was to switch to the left lane. We both sped straight ahead but now in opposite lanes. Fifty yards out, and he still didn't budge.

I eased off the gas as our cars converged. Slamming my breaks wasn't smart. I hoped he'd stay in his lane until we passed—nearer and nearer—thirty yards, twenty, ten . . . and I braced for impact. At the last second, the right corner of his hood veered inches toward me as if he'd woken up. I white-knuckled my steering wheel as we passed like hotrods playing daredevil. I was clear seconds later and didn't glance back to see if he'd figured out how close we'd each been to losing our lives. Then, I switched back into my right lane and continued forward. We'd survived by a whisker and only by the grace of God. Some minutes later, I recalled that I hadn't used my blinker when switching back into my proper lane. I didn't think I needed to self-report.

Thinking back on the narrow escape an entire decade later—realizing it had all happened in under a minute—I better understand how a lucky ant must feel after a human boot steps on ten of his buddies.

Almost Died Event # 15 – SPEEDING DRUNK– Age 45

I took my girlfriend, Teresa, to a Packers game. We had drinks afterward with her friends, Ty and Veronica. By nine p.m., we planned to grab a bite at a Broadway diner. I drove my Pontiac across the Walnut St. Bridge and the rail tracks. Sunday night traffic was sparse. Three vehicles were in line ahead of us at the stoplight across from a bank. We were talking, and I glanced at my side mirror. Glimmering lights reflected in the night sky. A pair of headlights came speeding over the bridge behind us, doing seventy. Two squad cars tailed the speeder. He continued straight toward us in the car line without evading traffic by shifting lanes. I shouted to Teresa to hold on. She half-turned as the rocket slammed into us, and we were plowed forward into the vehicles ahead. The simultaneous front-and-back collisions jerked us around in our seats. The seatbelts held, with no glass bursting from impact.

We sat stunned as the cops arrested the culprit. An ambulance arrived. We rolled the windows down and spoke with an EMT. I told her I was fine, but Teresa reported her neck had spasmed during the crash. The EMTs strapped her onto a longboard. My car needed towing, so I rode with them to the ER. I called Ty and Veronica to the hospital while Teresa was x-rayed. I explained how the accordion effect of the front cars absorbed the collision's energy. Still, Teresa and I could have been seriously injured or even perished if one of the fuel tanks had burst and trapped us in a multi-car fireball explosion. Teresa's neck spasms were minor. I heard weeks later that the driver was cited for his fifth DUI.

TENDERFOOT

Logline: When a young teen joins the Boy Scouts to camp and party with his friends one weekend, he learns survival skills mean more than winning a merit badge.

The judge glared down at me from behind his bench. His eyeglasses were steamed. His stern voice seethed with anger. "You stupid moron!" he barked with his forehead flushed. "Hundreds of innocent people could have died in that blaze—including your own careless ass!"

"Yes, Your Honor," I said meekly. I added, "But I never even made tenderfoot."

"What kind of lame excuse is that?"

"It's not an excuse," I replied. "Your Honor. Sir. It's simply a fact."

I confess to being a mischief-maker most of my life. Even at age twelve, I recall teasing my younger sisters by dangling our beloved pet tabby (Rick) over the open washing machine. My "black sheep" of the family claim-to-fame was getting caught by my father one night climbing on our house roof wearing only a dickie for a loincloth. I'd imagined I was an Indian scout scanning the moonlit terrain from a high bluff. This event occurred after my return home from my first and only Boy Scout jamboree.

Three of my close friends, led by my best friend Chopper, were all scouts. They convinced me to enlist as a rookie and accompany them on a weekend jamboree at Camp Bear Paw, which sits ninety miles due north of Green Bay. So join I did, and a week later, I wore a tan scout's shirt to my first camping event. Everyone was in high spirits. Our Troop 4 clumped along the wooded daylight path, reciting an exuberant marching chant. I was not yet a tenderfoot, but I tromped amid the bushes and towering trees with my comrades.

Our troop leader marched us in cadence, ordering me to: "Stay on the path, Mancheski. You'll be lost for a month if you miss a turn in these woods." He was correct. I possessed zero survival skills and couldn't spark a fire from dry twigs or rubbing rocks together. I was utterly useless. My sense of humor and joke-telling ability kept them from helicoptering me back home.

I couldn't sleep the first night in the bunk cabin. We were awakened sometime after midnight by wild hoots and hollering. A band of Indians attacked our camp. We fled through the woods, running for our scalps while they shouted and chased after us with hatchets. I had seen too many old Western movies to take the attack lightly. We dodged and shifted between the trees until finally reaching safety. I later learned the Order of the Arrow executed this invasion. They were a group of older scouts garbed and painted like Indian braves, so we were never under an actual attack.

I couldn't sleep the second night again in our cabin. I was stone-cold weary the following day. We were scheduled to go canoeing. Instead, my three friends and I sneaked around the lake and smoked cigarettes behind a cluster of high bushes. Chopper Lambert led us. We lit stick matches and carelessly tossed them onto leave clumps, stomping out the flames if they flared too high. Chopper and another boy carried lighters and flicked them on and off like hoods on a street corner. They sprayed lighter fluid on one flaming brush fire, causing the burning twigs and leaves to roar. I was standing too close and somehow got lighter fluid on my sock. In less than three seconds, my left foot burst into flames. I stomped around in a circle, yelling while trying to tamp down the flames with both hands. I instinctively knew it would take too long to sit down and remove my burning shoe and sock.

"Jump in the lake!" Chopper screamed like a high-pitched girl, but it was the best solution ever.

I hop-hobbled seven steps and long-jumped into the water. It was eight feet deep just off the shore, and being a weak swimmer—panicked besides—I sank straight down like a torpedo and felt my feet slide into the muddy weeds at the bottom.

More panic. I tried pushing off to resurface, but both feet were firmly in the muck. I'd already held my breath for a half-minute, but try as I might, I couldn't extract either foot free. With serious trouble mounting, I knew drowning was a reality. Yet a voice in my head (my guardian angel?) suggested twisting one stuck foot sideways instead of pressing downward. I took her advice, and it worked; I did the same with my other foot. With both legs free of the gripping weeds, I miraculously swam upward. Weighted by my soaked clothing, the water turned less murky as the surface neared. I finally popped my head above water, gasping, and my friends grabbed me by the arms and pulled me ashore.

I spent the rest of the day shivering and drying off, unable to shake the image of how close I'd come to drowning. Complaining about my singed ankle seemed irrelevant when I was lucky to be alive.

Although being young daredevils had been exhilarating, I hadn't even garnished a cooking badge. We packed our things on the third and final day and were driven back to Green Bay. I was a failure as a Boy Scout and informed our scoutmaster the following Monday of my resignation from the troop. I had failed to reach even the lowly rank of "Tenderfoot."

Two days later, word spread through our school that Camp Bear Paw had experienced a massive wildfire. It took combined firefighters from three counties to extinguish the blaze. The consensus was that it might have been started by errant Boy Scouts lighting leaf fires in the woods. Gulp.

I prayed that it had nothing to do with our smoking lark. But to this day, I picture our careless use of matches and lighters and the possibility we had somehow burned down half the Boy Scout camp, small towns, and nearby rural barns and homes. Gulp again.

I envisioned being brought before a judge in juvenile court and sentenced to a reform school for wayward young delinquents. *"You stupid moron! Hundreds of people could have died in that blaze—including your own careless ass!"* My only defense would be the sorry admission: "But, Your Honor, I never even made tenderfoot."

My nightmares persisted for over a week, still picturing the judge slamming his gavel and glowering down from his bench at me. The reform school sentence would last until age eighteen, when I could be safely released back into the community and the incident purged from my permanent record.

As you may have guessed, my experience as a Boy Scout proved less than fulfilling. I doubt my beige-shirted, badge-less image will ever appear on scouting recruitment posters.

Almost Died Event # 16 – DARK NIGHT TURNOFF – Age 46

One of my friends managed a downtown tavern called Coaches Corner. Kevin and his wife, Tera, both worked there. They invited me to a party at their condo in Suamico one Saturday night. My friend Exy came with me. We consumed beers and smoked weed at the party—which I seldom imbibed in due to brain fog. The party wound down. Exy told me he had friends waiting for him at another tavern. We bid our hosts goodbye. During the drive back to Highway 41, I pictured the entry ramp turnoff. The pot I'd smoked said otherwise. Anticipating the exit, I almost veered from the road into a deep culvert short of the freeway. It was a thirty-foot nosedive before crashing. At the last second, my beer brain overruled the hashish. I remained driving straight like nothing had happened. I sensed Exy's questioning look in the passenger seat. We yakked about the party as the proper turnoff appeared. Exy caught a ride back to Oconto later that night. I never told him how I'd come within whiskers of crashing us into oblivion.

DEATH BY HOE

Author's Note: The Almost Died Event #3, "Swing Blade," was revealed earlier. Below is the complete story.

Logline: When an athletic young teen is attacked by a crazed farmer next door, he discovers survival is a game of inches.

After a record-shattering run as the Sturgeon Bay High School football coach in 1959, Al Mancheski (my father) accepted a new head coaching position at Green Bay East High School—his old alma mater. He purchased a home on quiet, tree-lined Lawe Street, a block from St. Mary's of the Angels parochial school and parish. It was eight blocks from East High, the school he'd be coaching at when autumn rolled around in three months.

The family moved into the older home with a flourish in the summer of 1960. The five kids sprinted up and down the steps leading to the three bedrooms on the second floor and down the lower stairs into the shadowed basement. It was a gray-shingled, four-bedroom house with a broad, enclosed front porch. The kids occupied the top floor, with the parents in the first-floor main bedroom. The yard was narrow along the west side, with a sidewalk running the length of the house from the street and past the side entry door. The backyard held a string of four clotheslines, two apple and plum trees, and a cluster of current bushes growing behind the separated garage.

Being a lifelong athlete and award-winning football coach, Coach Al instilled his love of sports in his children. He erected a basketball backboard and hoop attached to the two-stall garage fronted by paved concrete. He also placed a seven-foot-high practice backboard in the spacious basement, where his three young boys, Jan, Mark, and Randy, could play basketball year-round.

While the situation seemed idyllic, it didn't take long before an unforeseen problem reared its sordid head. Next door to the family's new digs lived an elderly Polish couple. Old Mike Pubilski inhabited the compact next-door home and ruled his domain with an iron fist. Old Mike reigned over the drainage ditch between the two houses. He kept it clean of leaves, ice, snow, and other debris—running freely. This was due to the backyard vegetable garden that he fawned over like one would an only child. Old Mike hoed his garden constantly, weeding, seeding, and harvesting the bounty each autumn. He had a green thumb for gardening, but otherwise, he and his wife remained confined inside their house. The exception was the numerous hours the farmer spent inside his separate garage/shed in the backyard, which ran adjacent to the garden. There, he sharpened his variety of instruments and even polished his wheelbarrow.

Early each day, Old Mike faithfully attended 6 a.m. mass one block away at St. Mary's ornate Polish church. By this time, he was in his mid-sixties, and his stride had become a stiff-kneed shuffle. But it didn't stop him from keeping his grass mowed, raking the leaves blown into his yard, and, most of all, keeping his sidewalk pristine during the winter months of ice and heavy snowfall. These were but a few tasks, yet he excelled at them all. Rumor had it that he'd honed these skills while working on a large family farm in his youth.

It took only weeks before the new family seemed to get under their feisty neighbor's skin. As noted, the Mancheski family was a brood of budding athletes with Coach Al riding herd. The Pubilski couple, on the other hand, went quietly about their business. The missus was usually inside the house all day except when drying laundry on the outside clotheslines. Old Mike was either tending his garden or inside the secluded, dimly lit shed. Rarely did he deviate from his regimen. And all turned solemnly quiet during the chilly Wisconsin winter.

As the snow melted and winter turned to spring, both households became more active, with a deepening animosity rearing up again between the testy neighbors. Like prisoners suddenly freed from confinement, when not shooting basketballs at the driveway hoop, the Mancheski children booted soccer balls up and down their deep backyard or tossed footballs back and forth. They hit baseballs, softballs, and whiffle balls high into the air, with Coach Al teaching them to catch and throw properly. There were croquet mallets, metal hoops pressed into the lawn, daily kickball games, track sprints over hurdles, bicycles, skateboards, jump ropes, and rollerblades. A circus of constant activity. Young pitchers threw to masked catchers, all to the continuous shouts and the drum-pounding dribble of basketballs. The commotion occurred every day of the week, weather permitting.

As one might imagine, the constant racket was enough to drive a gruff-edged, older man—accustomed to years of privacy and quiet solitude—bonkers.

Old Mike's brooding nature finally got the better of him. Like predators defending their territory, a contest between the two clans soon evolved. Whenever one of the children's sports balls sailed from their yard onto the neighboring lawn, drainage ditch, or garden, a mad dash occurred between the elderly farmer bursting from his shed with a rake, garden hoe, or sickle in hand. He'd scoop up the invading ball while cursing, then scurry back inside his garage. There, he would destroy the offending object. Basketballs and footballs he stabbed and pierced until deflated; the harder baseballs, softballs, or croquet balls he would sharply hack at like Ed Gein until adequately butchered.

Coach Al, for his part, stayed out of the scrum. He once or twice exchanged words with Old Mike (in Polish) when the occasion arose, but mostly, he decided that his kids needed to learn to fend for themselves. They'd best avoid kicking or throwing balls into the next-door yard because, as the older man had insisted, wasn't it akin to trespassing? What if a neighbor, for instance, allowed their dog to run free and soil an adjacent yard? If it happened constantly, it would be intolerable, and tempers would flare.

Coach Al remained a neutral observer of the ongoing Cold War. His position was understandable due to his elevated stress levels from teaching high school all day and coaching football until six p.m. post-school. After that, there'd be strategy meetings with his assistant coaches. Thus, Coach Al arrived home in the evenings, bedraggled and weary. No doubt, the last thing he wanted to hear was how the grumpy old coot next door had captured a Spalding and destroyed it with a farm implement.

As the years passed and the children grew, a Battle Royale evolved between Old Mike, the farmer, versus Coach Al's eldest son, Jan. The boy had turned thirteen the past summer and grown into an agile and wiry young athlete. He played one sport after the next, constantly practicing in the backyard when not at team practices. And thus, the conflict's intensity grew. It featured the teenager's foot speed pitted against the irate farmer surging from his shed like a piranha, brandishing a weapon while charging toward an invading ball in his yard. Usually, the boy held the advantage by being the one who had booted or thrown the errant object. Yet the irascible neighbor never failed to respond when an offending invader landed on his property.

As the contest grew more heated, the situation for young Jan intensified. While the boy never egged on his older, cussing opponent—never bird-flipped him when surrendering a ball—he maintained his gloating attitude whenever outracing the executioner to the prize. On the other hand, Old Mike continued his colorful name-calling, whether successful or not. He would curse at the youngster: "*Effing count!* Sick little prick. Filthy *count* SOB." Or any number of other pejoratives aimed at demeaning the youthful athlete.

After barely rescuing a ball, the teenager would often slip into the family garage and peer out at the cunning old farmer. Considering this as mockery, Old Mike became even more enraged while pacing inside his low-lit shed. Jan studied his neighbor's odd behavior. Due to the number of close calls, he was determined to understand what type of psychopath he was dealing with.

As fate decided, young Jan would discover his answer on a quiet Friday afternoon in May. Basketball season was over. The snow melted, and the grass turned pasty brown to green. Walking home from school around 3:30 that afternoon, the boy decided the weather was warm enough to toss around a football outside. Because the nutcase neighbor had destroyed so many balls the past year, Jan's surplus of footballs had run low. Therefore, knowing he shouldn't but doing it anyway, he grabbed Coach Al's treasured trophy ball from its proud position atop the living room fireplace mantle. It was a tan-colored Duke pigskin, signed by the 1965 Packers NFL championship team. The award had been presented to Coach Al three months earlier when he'd been honored as the Wisconsin High School Football Coach of the Year.

Though the seventh grader understood the risk, Jan grabbed the football anyway. It's what teenagers sometimes do when they lack an understanding of how their actions might have negative consequences. The lad's intentions that day were noble. He was blowing off steam after school. One of Jan's favorite practice techniques when alone was lobbing a football about ten yards into the air and dashing forward to catch it before it landed. Cognizant of the trophy ball's value, his brain reminded him forcefully: *Do not let the ball hit the ground.*

Performing his technique alone in the backyard, Jan had accomplished the back-and-forth tactic about ten times before spying the farmer's dusky shadow through the window inside his garage. Yet, for whatever reason, the lad's common sense had lapsed. Closely studying the football he held, Jan could easily discern the famous signatures: *Jim Taylor, Bart Starr, Paul Horning, Jerry Kramer, Willie Wood* . . . and others. He read the more oversized scribble of Packers Head Coach Vince Lombardi near the ball's tan laces.

Pride and exuberance flooded the boy's veins. Jan was holding the signed Super Bowl Championship team in his hands. It felt like he was playing catch with the actual players, and gripping the pigskin transformed him into one of the world's luckiest young footballers. Subsequently—without thinking things fully through—he decided to try another of his warm-up tactics. Moving to face the house's back, fifteen yards away, Jan softly punted the football up onto the roof. The tiled surface was very wide and sloped down toward him. The football bounced erratically here and there before skipping down and dropping twenty feet over the edge. The boy snatched it as effortlessly as Max McGee.

Jan again felt infused with the Packers' championship glory. Multiple future Hall of Famers had signed the football—all living legends. He glowed with inner pride. He punted the orb again softly onto the roof, watching it pause, bounce, then skip down the incline and tumble over the edge. He again caught it effortlessly. It was all so pure and athletic that he caught himself grinning. After another three similar kicks and catches, Jan felt a deep inner peace settle in his chest—the way monks felt (he imagined) after meditating.

The urge to return inside the house swept over him. The reality of his actions was hitting home at last. Jan decided on one final boot-and-snag to keep his inner flame aglow. Being his final punt, he kicked the pigskin more solidly to ensure his efforts were meaningful. He cringed when the punt sailed left. For a crazy second, Jan pictured it striking the chimney. Instead, the ball took an errant bounce and skidded before beginning its descent. The football skidded down the roof and short-hopped against the aluminum gutter. The odd carom caused it to veer errantly toward the yard opposite, where the youth's eyes bulged while watching the football bounce four times before halting in the middle of the neighbor's back lawn—where it sat like a tossed hand grenade.

Jan's blood froze. The significance of his father's trophy ball rang louder in his head than a funeral knell.

Reality slapped him. The boy understood his dad would ground him until age thirty if he allowed the championship football to be captured by the maniac next door. Spurred by panic, Jan sprinted ten yards across his lawn, jumped the ditch, and beelined toward the brownish orb. At the same instant, the farmer burst from the shed's shadows carrying a long garden hoe while striding swiftly toward the football.

Both contestants converged on the nexus. Jan understood the race would be decided by milliseconds. Old Mike was approaching fast, wielding his lengthy weapon like an ax. The boy calculated his half-step advantage at getting to the football first. The older man likewise sensed this and double-gripped the garden hoe's long handle. Dipping and swooping like a halfback nearing the goal line, Jan scooped the ball up like a fumble. He felt the metal blade sweep over his skull. With the ball in hand, sprinting away, he glanced back at the farmer. Old Mike's swing had been so vicious that he'd pretzeled himself around like Hank Aaron whiffing at a Bob Gibson fastball.

Jan sped down the grassy path along the property's far side until emerging on the front sidewalk. The sleepy afternoon street was shaded and quiet. Panting from adrenaline, he carried the football tucked beneath his arm like he'd just returned a kickoff ninety-eight yards. Jan proceeded past his house and up the long driveway, where he vanished inside the family garage. His heart still tom-tommed in his chest. He peered across the lawn at Old Mike's shed. He could detect his enemy inside, head bobbing, pacing like a prisoner in his cell. The older man's curses carried through the open door, revealing frustration at his failed homicide attempt.

At this moment, Jan accepted how close he'd come to losing his life. The sharp blade could have easily fractured his skull, sliced cleanly through his jugular vein, or even pithed the back of his neck, causing instant paralysis. Instead, it had passed over his head by what he guessed was a centimeter. Coach Vince Lombardi's gravelly voice in his head now proclaimed: "Gentlemen, I've said it many times before—football is a game of inches."

A half-hour later, perched upstairs on the edge of his bed, Jan twitched like an epileptic. The image of his bleeding teenage body lying dead on the neighbor's lawn was vivid. His imagination ran an inner movie: Watching Old Mike—as if costumed now as serial killer Ed Gein—hovering over his silent corpse. His eyes surveyed the neighborhood for witnesses. Then the homicidal maniac dragged the young victim by the ankles into his shadowy garage, where he'd butcher the boy's body the same way he'd mutilated over fifty of their sports balls. Slicing his enemy up would be simple. Jan guessed the sturdy farmer had butchered hundreds of calves, sheep, and hogs before, many far outweighing his teenage corpse. Of course, if any cops arrived, Old Mike would deny everything. He'd been inside his shed all afternoon and hadn't seen or heard anything unusual. If the officers pressed him, he'd lapsed into broken Polish and brush them aside the way horsetails shoo away annoying flies.

Shaking his head to dissolve these images, Jan listened as his dad's station wagon pulled into the driveway and parked inside the garage. Remaining on his bed's edge, he heard fifteen minutes of his sister's back-and-forth chatter downstairs. They were setting the dinner table as their mom issued orders. Pots and pans rattled. Jan detected the aroma of sauerkraut and spareribs infiltrating the house. It made him think of butchered hogs, and he forced the violent imagery to dissolve.

Jan understood that the clever play was reporting the incident to his father before they gathered at the dinner table. Exiting his bedroom, he descended the stairs and located Coach Al sitting in the living room's corner rocker. The newspaper was spread across his lap. Remaining standing, Jan relayed what had happened, emphasizing how close he'd come to losing his life only an hour ago. He dryly reported the incident like the detectives on the Dragnet TV show—"Just the facts, son."

Coach Al listened in his chair. He remained mostly silent. He kept his cool as usual when listening to his son's tall tales about how countless different football, basketball, and baseball contests had unfolded.

Finally, when Jan explained how his near-death episode had transpired, Coach Al set aside the sports page and listened with more interest. He said, "So, you're telling me he didn't grab another football to puncture, right?"

Jan knew the truth must be revealed, void of embellishment. "Yes, sir. But it was a very close call. I was playing catch by myself with your Packers ball (turning his head) on the mantle there. You know? Flipping it in the air and catching it?" He exhaled. "I was bringing it back inside when a wasp buzzed me. It made me miss the ball, and it bounced into Pubilski's yard."

Well aware of the ongoing feud, Coach Al's eyes narrowed. He rose from the lounger to the fireplace mantle. He plucked the football down and closely examined it. The leather appeared scratched and scuffed, with many players' names barely readable. He lifted his eyes and stared tightly at his son. "How did the signatures get messed up?"

Jan swallowed hard, owning up: "I punted it onto the roof once or twice, Dad. You know? Catching it before landing?" He quickly added, "I dreamed of playing in the championship game. You know? Like Don Chandler?"

The disappointment was etched across Coach Al's face. He squinted tightly at his son. "You know those roof tiles are made of asphalt pebbles, don't you?"

"I was thinking about the championship game," Jan repeated. "And the players who signed your football." The boy's eyes glistened, knowing how lame his explanation sounded.

"And now half their names are smudged off." In frustration, Coach Al set the scuffed football back on the mantlepiece. The racket from the kitchen had died down, and Jan heard his younger brothers clomp down from upstairs. Mom's voice echoed from the kitchen, "Al. Jan. Dinner's ready."

The odor of sauerkraut filled the house. Coach Al shook his head, then instead of cuffing him, he placed his arm around his son's shoulders. He said, "You know I'm pissed off, right?"

"I'll . . . try buying a new one. Maybe at the Packers Pro Shop?"

His dad sighed as if exhausted by the entire affair. "Like I always tell you," he said fatherly, "it's not a sin if you didn't mean to do it on purpose."

"Yes, sir," Jan said sheepishly, wondering if he'd dodged a second bullet in an hour.

They stepped together into the kitchen and sat on their usual chairs. His siblings were already seated, chatting merrily. Putting the final mashed potato bowl on the table with a hot pad beneath it, their mother finally sat down.

Coach Al's voice overrode the table chatter. He announced:

"Jan's going to say the dinner prayer tonight. I hope we're all thankful that we're here together." The other family members glanced at one another in mild confusion.

With his eyes downcast, Jan said reverently, "Bless us, O Lord, for these thy gifts, which we are about to receive . . ."

While enjoying their pork and sauerkraut dinner, their father said nothing more about the incident. Blocking out the family's chit-chat, Jan's active imagination again took flight. He felt the sharp metal blade *whoosh* breezily, violently mere centimeters over his buzzcut hair. A close shave. Or in baseball lingo, when a fastball zips past your ear: "You got a haircut, sonny. Didn't ya?"

Silently at the family dinner, Jan gnawed on a pork hock, mixing it with kraut and mashed potatoes. While he chewed and swallowed appreciatively, he considered how lucky he was. An image formed in his head:

"*DEATH BY GARDEN HOE,*" the local newspapers would have headlined the affair. He again pictured his dead body lying on the neighbor's bloody lawn. Jan imagined two patrolmen leading the handcuffed killer by the elbows toward their car. Walkie-talkies cackled, and more squad cars arrived by the minute. Dispatch would announce that the meat wagon was on its way. Old Mike, of course, would mumble and curse at them all, explaining how the young trespasser had deserved his comeuppance.

While remorseful that his dad's prized football had been ruined, young Jan realized how fortunate he was to be still breathing. What struck the lad even greater was how calmly his father had accepted the reality of his most cherished award being nearly destroyed. He hadn't thrown a screaming fit, threatened divine retribution, or even laid into his eldest boy about how careless he'd been. And though relieved, Jan couldn't shake away the reality of his stupidity that afternoon. It somehow made the episode of his nearly being murdered feel even worse.

Author's Note: As the years passed, I appreciated my dad's ability to go with the flow that day. There'd been no screaming or shouting about things that couldn't be fixed or remained beyond anyone's control. Reflecting back on the day that I had almost been murdered, perhaps the most significant lesson I gained from my father was the ability to stay calm during a crisis. Although I never got around to looking into purchasing a replacement for Coach Al's 1965 Championship football, which I'd regretfully ruined, I continue to recall the incident as vividly as if it happened yesterday.

Almost Died Event # 17 – JOY OF HYDROPLANING – age 48.

I worked checking patients' eyes in Shawano on a March Saturday. It was one of those strange Wisconsin weather days where the sun shone, but fifteen minutes later came a downpour. After finishing work mid-afternoon, I drove back to Green Bay. Sunlight glared off the pavement, yet the road showed spots of dampness that reflected like an oil sheen. The sign read: Pulaski 15 miles. I drove my gray Audi coupe up an incline in sight of a large car dealership. Navigating down the slope, I was going an easy seventy-five. Traffic flowed in the opposite direction but was absent on my side. The radio played the Wisconsin Badgers station. While zipping into the right-hand lane, I suddenly lost control of the steering. The road's downslope maintained my speed. When it flattened, I realized my tires were locked in a hydroplane skid across the damp pavement. Everything slowed inside the car. I knew enough not to oversteer. The radio announcers babbled away as I whisked along Highway 29. Only God's hand guided me. In the rearview mirror, I saw a semi come up the ramp behind me. He'd assessed my situation and stayed far behind. I continued sliding forward at 70 mph. The road ahead glistened in the sun like a mirage. The pavement shimmered as I floated along, a surfer riding a wave.

Time was locked in dreamlike slow motion. I was fascinated by how the radio announcers were talking in natural tones. I considered silencing the radio while floating between life and death, yet some inner voice reminded me: "Never interfere with destiny." A minute later (feeling like ten), I felt the steering wheel re-sync with the tires. Yet I remained a helpless participant if they suddenly gripped the concrete road and the Audi flipped multiple times through the air before careening from the road.

I gripped the steering wheel, and navigation returned to my hands. I eased the car down to sixty-five, then sixty. The worst part had passed. The radio duo continued discussing the Wisconsin Badgers wrap-up. I remained in my lane, exhaling slowly. I thanked my Guardian Angel Toni for saving me and promised to bring the Audi in for new tires on Monday.

OTHER POEMS

MY FINAL BREATH (note: repeated earlier in "Murdered" story)

The end is nigh.
I lay at the point of death in extremis,
Dying, moribund, critical, dire,
At death's door, perishing, fading fast.
Near the end now, expiring, forfeiting the ghost.
Sinking shriveled on my deathbed inside withered skin.
Foundering, doomed, my faint breaths counting down.
On my last legs, both feet planted in my mortal grave.
Raspy half-breaths, I'm at rope's end and eating lead,
Jerked by slugs from God's Gatling gun.
Terminal, a disintegrating husk, fey and succumbing to
Life's ultimate final act. My soul waves the white flag in
Surrender, amplifying my frailty. My ship sinks, decayed,
Expiring and sliding deeply toward Davey Jones' locker.
I wallow in self-despair—farewell to those not bedside.
My eyes close, and lips exhale death's final sigh.
My ghost stumbles stiffly toward the beckoning
Tunnel of light that floats above or is flat—I'm unsure.
Postscript:
Too late, I'm sure, but Lord, please forgive me for my sins.

WRITER'S FRUSTRATION

When you think you're done, you're but halfway home,
That's how most stories go.
When composing books or scripts, or tunes,
It's the wasted time that blows.

WARRIOR ANT

There is no braver ant than Zada,
For Zada will rule the clan.
And those who kneel to honor Zada
Will know sanctity and love.
For Zada will rule the clan,
And his legions will conquer all.
Spreading colonies far and wide
For those kneeling in his thrall.
Zada visits Ant Queen's chamber,
Where a million soldiers be born.
Seeking sanctity and renown
Until Shadow Hawk swoops down.
Attacking Zada and his warrior ranks,
Evil Hawkbird wipes them clean.
Shows no sanctity or love,
Then, he escapes back up above.
Yet, Ant Queen in her hive is spared,
And Zada's reborn a warrior.
His legions attack in a mighty swarm
To avenge the hawkish deadly storm.
Shadow Hawk is slain and carried back,
To feed the clan for what they lack.
Warrior Zada is now Lord and King.
His pincher fists hold a mighty swing.
Then Ant Queen one day devours Zada;
No sanctity, love, just she-bitch pow-a.
And the colony lives on as before.
Until warrior Zada is born once more.

Author's Note: Here's a joyous little sonnet to brighten your day, put a smile on your face, and send you on your merry way.

VOODOO HEX

Wind and waves crash rocky shores,
A launching midnight rocket's roar.
Liberia by moonlight—voodoo's core.
Stone compound on a tall third-floor
Drips blood from walls by witchy hand.
The feathered priest kneels in a ritual stance,
Writes your lasting tombstone's name—
In blood upon his parchment page.
Like a falcon perched at a silver bowl,
Candles flicker, and black shadows stroll
Across the room to leap and dance,
His vulture beak is a savage lance.
Weep bloody streaks and stinking mess—
Whose entrails cast disgusting stench.
On a ceiling high with crimson signs,
Spells out your name in his design.
Red streaks across his dark chest glow,
Eyes stare from the snarling mask of bone.
Pours infant blood from the chalice lip,
On a gemstone while his whispers slip.
Hurls curses at your loved ones thus,
Whose bones will burn to charry dust.
Hearts oozing bloody chambers glee,
Your fatal name in blood writes he.
More scarlet bowl leaps up in flame,
Twin arrows guide red pinpricks aim,
At those who read this tome by night,
Twin eyes behind the bone-mask fright.
With an evil grin, he knows your name,
Lights parchment with his note aflame.
Drops burning in his bowl to curse—
And sends your way his charnel hearse.

With gnashing teeth and a sinister smile,
That twists behind his mask of vile.
Red prick-pins staring scarlet eyes,
Reflections seen with no disguise.
Stares up at you, dear reader, and his
Spell flies at you while wickedly whispers.
Your end aloud—the last die cast—and
His cackling shriek is a lunatic's laugh.

FINAL POSTSCRIPT REGARDING *BIG GIANT PUBLISHER* CENSORSHIP:

I want to thank all the kind readers who purchased my series books and the gracious and outstanding reviewers who gave my novels so many favorable reviews on all the various book review platforms and sites. May you all experience happiness, joy, and prosperity in the many years ahead.

Warmest Regards, JM

Update Note: While penning these words on September 10, 2023, my books and I remain banned across the BIG GIANT PUBLISHER platform—this despite my being a long-time and active Premium Purchase Member. I remain labeled as a "deviant, devious, rabble-rouser of a novelist, whose books and stories must be silenced for the good of humanity and to help preserve the sanctity of the universe. "So help us, God!" (as sentenced by BGP's AI-bot Deputy).

** Whom, ironically, I imagine to be quite the confirmed atheist.

Final Note: I sometimes joke that if a job title were designed: "Reader for a living," I'd be a millionaire. I thank my mother, Dawn, for teaching me to read via picture books at the tender age of three. And I've never stopped. I confess that I currently possess nearly a thousand books inside my house. They fill the basement, living room bookshelves, and boxes in various closets and garages. At times, I feel like a hoarder. I'll one day donate them for other readers' enjoyment, but for now, I confess that they're all like old dear friends to me. I'll keep them around for a while, referring to them when I recall specific passages I've enjoyed over the years. This stated, I hope you've gained some modest pleasure while reading these tales. And here's to hoping we all stay far away from as many future ADEs as possible.

— JM (drjjjjdr@yahoo.com)

Website: jansonmancheski.com

FB site: Janson Mancheski Author

FB site: Janson Mancheski Books

www.ingramcontent.com/pod-product-compliance
Lightning Source LLC
Chambersburg PA
CBHW030009290326
41934CB00005B/278

9781950316335